CHANNELLED MESSAGES
FOR THE WORLD TODAY

Linda Matamani
Beulah Sai Kumari

authorHOUSE®

AuthorHouse™
1663 Liberty Drive
Bloomington, IN 47403
www.authorhouse.com
Phone: 1-800-839-8640

Published by AuthorHouse 10/21/2014

ISBN: 978-1-4969-4463-4 (sc)
ISBN: 978-1-4969-4462-7 (hc)
ISBN: 978-1-4969-4464-1 (e)

Library of Congress Control Number: 2014918256

CHANNELLED MESSAGES
FOR THE WORLD TODAY

Contents

Introduction to this book

The texts in this book are channelled messages received from the spiritual world.

The *spiritual world* has a higher frequency than the Earth and is therefore more suffused with light.

This particular light of a higher frequency is not merely light but contains high levels of consciousness.

One possibility of this level of consciousness is the *White Brotherhood,* which is a group of *Ascended Masters.*

At present the *Ascended Masters* are directing the Earth especially through the evolutionary process for which it is now designated.

The Masters who have ascended to the spiritual realms, all, with a few exceptions, lived on Earth. They know what it is like to be in a human body, they are aware of our emotions and understand the polar effects here on planet Earth.

A number of these spiritual masters have formed a *Karmic Council* and guide Mother Earth from their higher realms of Light. The messages from the *Karmic Council* to the people living in these times of change are contained in this book.

For the reader, it is a 'Message' which serves as a guide and explanation to comprehend the next few years on Earth. The texts contain information which increases the readers' awareness through the inherent energies.

This book serves as an explanation for the mind, and at the same time it is energy which increases the awareness of every reader.

ALL texts in this book are medial messages and come from the *spiritual world* of the *Ascended Masters*.

This introduction has been given by Master Saint Germain.
He was and is the initiator of this 'Message'.

Introduction by Master Saint Germain

I AM MASTER SAINT GERMAIN
I greet you in the terrestrial light!

This book needed to be written for the new era, for the energy of the Fifth Dimension.

The light will be more brilliant and the sun will shine more brightly on planet Earth - Gaia.

The air will be fluffy and light, and so should your life be too.

Using your thoughts, you can shape time and space.

Do you need time, imagine it, do you need more space, create it. It is an exercise of the mind, which can be realised through the heart centre.

Imagine, and so it will be.

Have the courage to practically implement the theory of thinking, thus together you will all create the "Golden Age".

This book is the manual to practice creativity.

Trust and believe in yourself, and you will succeed.

This is Saint Germain,
the Ascended Master of the Violet Flame of Transformation.

You, reading this book, are being initiated into the new energy and will be free for ever.

Life needs to be redefined: what is happiness, what is joy, what is life?

You are one with all that is.

You are the creator of your new world, you are 'Divine'.

Act according to the great will of God.

Take responsibility for your thoughts, actions and creations to the benefit of all beings living on Earth, to the benefit of all the elements and to the benefit of the great soul – Gaia.

This book is intended as a guide for your future.

Your actions serve your freedom and your ascent into the 5th Dimension.

It is now time to alter the way you think; get ready for the energy messages which I am sending here from the higher realms of the spiritual world.

I am Master Saint Germain. I greet you in the terrestrial light.

Information concerning the origin of the texts: the channels

A channel allows energy and information from the spiritual realms of the universe to flow through. This information often takes the form of messages/texts or of energy patterns which can be sensed and felt.

In this book, two soul siblings have been asked by Master Saint Germain to work together. Due to this team work, the energy of the texts in this book is very luminous.

The messages are unique in that

- the channel Matamani received the text from the ascended masters of the *Karmic Council* as messages in written form,
- the channel Sai Kumari received the messages in the form of energy by translating the texts from German into English.

Through their cooperation, both channels have exponentially elevated the texts and energy of this book.

Two soul sisters were brought together by Master Saint Germain to bring this energy work to Earth.

In great love, the Karmic Council thanks the channels for their team work.

Helios, the sun god, guides into the 5th Dimension

Helios is a high spiritual presence of light of the new energy. He introduces the new era on Earth. He radiates the white ray of light.

The 5th Dimension is taking place on Earth. There is an increase in energy, which makes the change difficult for mankind. Matter, the dense environment in which you people move, will visibly change in substance and appearance. The colours will be more brilliant and intense, the sun will appear noticeably brighter. The filter of the eye chakra will become thinner, whereby the body will absorb more energized light and the oscillation of the body cells will change. During the changeover period, which begins now, many people will complain of muscular tension and pain, which will disappear again. To facilitate and accelerate the reduction of tension, it is recommended to regularly drink magnesium dissolved in plenty of water. The nerves transport the frequencies of light more rapidly through the body, through the cells. Magnesium enhances the conductivity of all cells and the flow rate of the nerve cells. Magnesium water helps the body to rid itself of the tension faster.

The increasing tension in the body makes many people feel uncertain about what is happening to them.

Conventional medicine cannot do much. This results in a lack of understanding as to what is happening to the human body. The pressure in the cells increases and the lack of understanding turns into anger and aggression. This serves to balance the tension in the body and as such it should be understood. To alleviate the tension, magnesium water, walks in nature and light physical exercise are recommended.

Easily digestible food and plenty of rest strengthen the body and reduce the tension quickly.

The increased frequency of light effects a change in matter. Building materials such as stones, metals and plastics change their molecular weight and can be used more and more easily and flexibly. The strength of the material does not suffer. The increased molecular weight of the old building materials enables new possibilities for design. The flexibility of the materials increases and resists wind, rain and sun rays more effecttively. Decay due to weathering is no longer possible. Houses built with materials of increased molecular weight reflect in the sunlight. Houses of old building materials adapt or fall apart. Resistance in building materials is only provided by flexible material.

In the future, people will prefer to live only in houses with a higher vibration because it balances and harmonizes the body. Houses made of mud and wood have an increased light permeability and therefore a high degree of flexibility. Old houses can stand the test of time while new houses break down.

Building materials that can be recycled and biodegradable materials are the building materials of the future. Cement as an adhesive should quickly change. A bio-material from plants should be added to increase the vibration, and hence the flexibility. Only in this way will cement remain a suitable construction adhesive and be able to survive the new era.

The tension of the increased light also affects the plant world. New plants which can implement the new light better will evolve. Old plants where the cell structures are too dense, will die. Trees, such as birch and willow species, adapt to the light quickly and their cell structure is flexible. Trees with very large, dense cell structures, such as oaks and chestnuts, are increasingly afflicted with diseases and will die off slowly. Changes in the plant world will take place at an increased pace in the years ahead. Flowers, for example, will bloom longer and produce larger blooms. This is brought about by the new light of the sun.

In the nucleus, crops, fruits and vegetables, and even fodder will bear a higher energy, and thus energize the bodies of humans and animals more effectively. There will be less food and fodder because less will be required. The body will be saturated faster and still be well supplied with the nutrients it needs. About 50% of the current arable land will be able to supply the entire world with sufficient energy. At present already all herbs form part of Energy Food.

Blooms, especially, should be consumed because the increased frequency of light in them supports the human cells in the process of transformation. The consumption of herbs accelerates the reduction of stress in the human body. Many plants with a high nutrient content will appear. All so-called 'weeds' have already adapted to the high light frequency. They help the body to heal within a short period.

'Weeds', i.e. wild herbs, should be researched and specified soon for they will help to bring about the balance in the human body. Depending on the composition of the soil, wild herbs have various ingredients, and as such must be recognised.

Healing teas, made from herbs, are very important for the harmony in the bodies of humans as well as animals during this period of transition. They balance the tension in the cells quickly.

Today already, naturally grown fruit is light nourishment for the body and aids cell regeneration within a short time. The sweetness of fruit activates the insulin metabolism in the body, which stimulates cells to vibrate at a higher frequency. The human body thereby heals itself and automatically adjusts to the high frequencies of light.

Due to the transition into the 5th Dimension, life on your planet changes.

The hustle, bustle and stress decrease. You will be more relaxed and more balanced.

Will, the strong power of volition, changes. Will no longer dominates your mind. You are able to 'just be'. For your everyday life this implies living according to the needs of your soul. The excessive and unbridled physical dominance stops. In your bodies, your soul and spirit live consciously and direct it so that it is satisfied with food, drink, exercise, care, and caress. The soul-spirit wishes to live in an attractive home, namely the body, and will shape it accordingly.

The soul-spirit determines the body's age and appearance. The body is designed according to the aims of the soul. The cells follow the soul-spirit and form accordingly.

The aging process may be abolished totally. Aging is no longer necessary.

The process of dying as you know it today, will no longer be necessary. Being aware of your multidimensionality you will choose the time to leave your body. In dialogue with the body, you (your soul-spirit) determine when the change 'death' is at hand. This is what you also do now, but unconsciously. In a few years' time, people will begin to make this decision consciously and openly. As a result, many souls will contemplate the possibility.

Sick and worn out bodies in particular can be vacated faster and without a long process of suffering.

Awareness increases rapidly and therefore also the understanding of the interrelationships of body-mind-spirit.

The body is the 'home', the 'seat' of the soul here on earth.

The material body is also needed in the 5th Dimension. The Earth is still dependent on matter; it will not be a pure spirit-planet. The 5th Dimension, too, remains material, but can be changed more easily and quickly. Currently you are still living in density and rigidity; there is too much matter. From year to year this changes faster and faster. By means of your consciousness, the spirit, your spirit, changes your body, your thinking, everything. You will be surprised what you will be thinking then. Thoughts are the first thing to change in many people during this year already. When the body tension has eased, you will be surprised about your own thoughts. Your thoughts will be gentler and quieter. Aggression will have departed from your thoughts. You will be more aware of yourself and less fixated on others.

The thought 'what do others think and believe about me' is no longer necessary. Your true nature evolves and you concentrate on your own progress.

Your personality strengthens and shapes rapidly. Everyone is aware of their abilities and advances them.

The shaping process triggered by the mind reaches all age groups. Old people who welcome this change will thereby prolong their lives and reshape them. All people, young and old, wish to participate in the great change on Earth. Before your consciousness unfolds completely, you will feel that something is changing. This feeling will trigger a process of self-exploration. Only then will you 'meet' your consciousness. It will 'introduce' itself to you and teach you. The training will take place via your thoughts, because you will be wondering, 'what am I thinking now'. This is how your spiritual teacher, your own consciousness, works with you.

This training within yourself, this thought - spirit - consciousness, is the crucial approach of change in regard to the ascent into the 5th Dimension, and for the profound social change within all nations. This is the only way this process of change will succeed. Change always begins with the individual. Thereafter all, or a group, will change society. Society is very inert; a new group awareness is required. This develops fastest with children and adolescents.

At first the educational systems should be adapted speedily. In the old system, children imitate the adult world. There is no room for individuality and independent creativity. Currently, students are standardized and passed through school like robots.

In this power system 'school', many children are sick. We and you need the children to reshape society on Earth, which will not work with children and adolescents who are ill. Liberal thinking is not alive any longer, and this should change quickly.

(I deliberately chose the negation 'not' in the text to jolt you, to show that you urgently need to change your systems.)

The 'storage sites' for little children need to be changed first. Parents should have the freedom to choose from all options. During the first years of their lives, the parents can take the great responsibility of taking care of their children themselves. Your daycare centres need very conscientious educators who live highly ethical and responsible lives, and who pass these on too. And also the schoolteachers should be very conscientious people with high ideals. Teachers and educators are the first adjusting screws to guide your society onto the path of liberation towards the new era. The children and adolescents already feel the oncoming energy and are looking forward to it. Help them implement it in everyday life. In some respects, the anthroposophic schools may serve as models for public schools. It takes courage and perseverance in the implementation.

The children of the new era have already come to Earth with a heightened awareness and a quick mind, and this should be taken into account in class. The rules and content of learning should be more specific and individual. The affinities must be recognised and intensified. A basic knowledge may be sufficient for students. What really matters, in the future and actually now already, is the promotion of the specific dispositions of each child, which should be encouraged, individually. Adults need to realise this in order to change the systems.

Already, children show their dissatisfaction and lack of challenge by abnormalities in their behaviour. Many incarnated (reborn) children souls are pure, to whom disharmony is foreign and physically painful.

Schools can be places of encounter and exchange in a peaceful environment. Teachers should be aware of this and act accordingly. Here special instruction and training of teachers are required.

The state of consciousness of every human being is the most important point to change society.

Life, your family, and your work will change rapidly in the next 3 to 5 years.

The hustle and bustle of everyday life will gradually disappear. You will be given more time. The indrawing spiral of time expired in December 2012. From January 2013, what you regard as time is developing into a great spiral again.

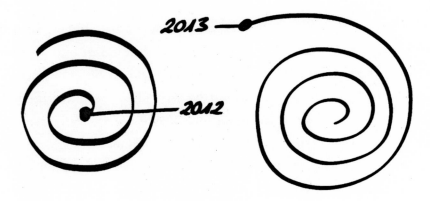

Due to this change, stress will be reduced immediately and a day will feel longer. The routine of the day will proceed in a calmer manner. This enables you to take more time for yourself. For a few minutes each day, just sit down, do nothing, just gaze - do not even think. This will change the range of vision and perspective on your actions, and will result in a new way of viewing things. Due to the peace and the 'altered' time factor, there will be more communication within the family. This smoothens out conflicts because no pressure arises during the conversation. Resulting from the peace within every individual, communication proceeds from the energy of the heart. Thanks to the new way of interacting with each other in conversation, you immediately change the vibration of your heart and pluck up the courage to be authentic and to speak the truth. This will first take place within the family. All family members have a genuine interest in communicating from the heart chakra.

Consequently, many things will sort themselves out automatically. People who see each other daily, live or work together, will adapt to a mutual frequency quickly. Contrary to now, misunderstandings, not understanding what the other says, will no longer be the order of the day. Understanding each other will be reinforced, as well as the pleasure of communicating - conversing at soul level, emanating from the heart.

With individuals changing within their families, this will also be conveyed outward. This change will slowly come to pass within the workplace as well as in public life. Communication, speaking the truth, will endure. Within a conversation, falsehood will be exposed and recognized as such. The aspect of truth, truthfulness, will be very decisive in the new era. Once lies are unmasked, peace will prevail.

Lies and manipulation reduce a person's light energy, and this low vibration causes physical pain. The transfer of energy will be regulated in the same way. Those who purify themselves and are truthful, will be able to integrate the light energy into the system of the body well. Those who remain stuck in the old patterns will perceive pain due to the opacity of their bodies. The more permeable and flexible the human body is, the more light it can absorb.

The old patterns include lies, manipulation, fraud, taking advantage, and much more. Owing to the refining and clarifying process, each person can cleanse themselves in a short time and be ready for the absorption of light in the cells. The cleansing process of the mind is very important. The body too should be cleansed. Drinking lots of water and abstaining from alcohol, drugs, tablets and chemically treated foods are part of physical cleansing. Taking walks in windy weather, which is what you will have, will cleanse your aura and relieve you of energies which are not yours. Sauna and brushing the body support the cleansing process in a gentle way. Herbal teas and fasting support the body to rid itself of waste.

The clarifying process includes the cleaning of homes, gardens, clothing and much more. Cleansing at all levels, both inside and out.

Working conditions change rapidly. Companies will be restructured to the benefit of employees. Power play will dissolve. More importance will be attached to cooperation. The authentic outward appearance of companies is strengthened only by the inherent equality and sovereign styles of leadership. People will avoid contracts with manipulative and power-oriented banks, insurance companies etc. Again, truthfulness and reliability prevail. Supply and demand will rapidly be restructured and adapted. When, within the energy field, you can distinguish lies from the truth, many things will sort themselves out quickly. Your market economy supports this process of conversion.

During the phase of transformation, the monetary system will still be maintained. Since money helps you enter into the processes of learning very quickly, money is still needed. Once all the processes of transformation have been completed worldwide, the finance market, and thus the people, will decide that it will be easier to abolish money.

But this will take some time.

At present, you find yourselves at the beginning of a great process of cleansing which brings about many changes. All public systems will change. In offices and administrations power structures will be abolished. Even executives participate in the great cleansing processes and change as a result. Due to inactivity and pain, many people will stay away from work in the near future. Consequently, systems of administration and business will collapse. That which has no continuance, no resistance, has to be restructured and reorganized. Readjustment is inevitable. This also affects your political power structure. Politics, like all administrations and institutions, work to maintain and enlarge their systems, which is the power game. This should change as soon as possible.

Citizens are entitled to have a say. You determine how taxpayers' money is used (the learning process of money). The current worker participation is a policy of paternalism.

Politics and administration should serve citizens and act in the interests of the latter. Now citizens are helpless and this is how they face the machinery of political power (politics, public authority). Defend yourselves and make the wheeling and dealing of these institutions transparent. The permeability of and the insight into the political and administrative systems will change them. Here too, clarification and cleansing will help. You will transform these systems which rule over you. Your political system is very cumbersome because it is entirely subjected to the power structure. Indeed, every politician is power-oriented and wants to remain that way. It remains to be seen how quickly the transition to a peaceful, liberal system will succeed. An alteration in thinking and doing is necessary. Politicians too are people of your era, and are personally involved in the cleansing processes of the new energies. Thus there is hope that every politician will change.

We from the spiritual world support your efforts, and channel the new energies into the political arena too.

Public life too is subject to the changes already taking place.

The media, whether they like it or not, will turn to the truth. This makes your news more truthful and transparent. This change in the media has already started. Many people who work in this field are interested in spreading the truth.

Television ratings and newspaper sales allow the propagation of lies. With the distinction between truth and lies, the manipulation is revealed here too. The more you follow your intuition, the faster you will recognize the truth and thus expose the manipulation. The media will change quickly once they have recognised this trend. Here the learning field of money is still required because profits are a great incentive for media companies. However, the media institutions will convert their reports and broadcasts. In the future, you will be able to filter information for the new era and apply it in everyday life. The truth of reports will prevail.

Radiating brilliant, divine light, Helios takes leave with an exercise in perception - God be with you.

An exercise in recognizing the truth:

- ➢ *Close your eyes and breathe deeply, twice.*
- ➢ *Visualize bright light surrounding you; you are standing in brilliant light.*
- ➢ *You seek an answer: formulate the question or visualize the situation.*
- ➢ *Does the brilliant light surrounding you remain unchanged, or does it change – take note.*
- ➢ *If a change in the light occurs, the truthfulness is questionable.*
- ➢ *If the light surrounding you remains unchanged, truth prevails.*
- ➢ *Breathe deeply and return to your wakeful state.*

Master Saint Germain speaks about cleansing and transformation

This is Master Saint Germain speaking to you through the Violet Flame of Transformation.
The time has come for each one to clarify and purify themselves.

The past, leave that behind you, and look ahead now. Events from the past, allow them to pass. Do not linger on them in thought.

When you have purified and clarified yourselves, the past is no longer of any importance for the future. The new quality of time only registers the moment. The 'Now' becomes important.

Past experiences are stored in your cells and are called your cellular memory. It can always be recalled via your feelings. What is important now is to be clear in thought and deed.

The idea, the vision that you are seated on a glass chair and that the Violet Flame is ablaze beneath you, and that it is flooding and thus cleansing your aura (the body of light surrounding you) as well as every cell, is a good exercise to clarify burdens of the past. Do this exercise daily, and you will feel the cleansing and relief in your mental body (the aura layer in which feelings and emotions are seated). In this way, you quickly clear yourselves of your burdens as well as of those which usurp you. Conflicts and pressures are thus resolved. You no longer need these old behavioural patterns for the future.

Let go of them!

It is unimportant with whom you had conflicts or arguments, or what these were about. After the process of clarification, you will be able to look everyone in the eye. Everything is fine the way it is now.

Past problems which weigh you down, cast them off like an old backpack and give thanks for the ease which you now experience. Only those who are free and light enter the 5th Dimension.

Therefore clarify all your relationships and circumstances. Make peace with your conflicting thoughts. Clarify your feelings such as anger and inferiority, now. All people on planet Earth are affected by this cleansing process.

The 5th Dimension can only be achieved with peace, clarity and an increased awareness.

The energies and radiations from the universe onto the Earth set this clarification process in motion within all people. Whoever resists, remains rooted in their old patterns of behaviour and will not enter into the new age.

It is possible to stick to the old structures. The ascent into the new era is voluntary, nobody will be forced. For the old inert structures a dimension similar to your present world will be created. For learning purposes, it will be possible for the old behavioural patterns to persist here. Here physical problems, pain and stress will be experienced.

Everyone can decide for themselves. The upliftment into the new era brings a lot of freedom for each of you.

Responsibility, personal responsibility for your actions is a prerequisite for the transition. Human beings are expected to participate in shaping and creating the new dimension.

This creativity is possible and can be implemented only if everyone is aware of the responsibility for their actions, towards themselves and others. The concepts of ethics, morality and justice are practised by many of you now already. But it would seem that this happens on a voluntary level.

In the new era, which started as early as 2012, these virtues are a basic requirement for shaping society. Those who live very responsibly, are free. Freedom means letting go of guilt, leaving it behind you. The ritual of forgiveness cleanses all burdens and entanglements in relationships. Forgiveness which comes from the heart brings healing to all your relationships and to your body.

Do try to understand this!

Those who wish to heal themselves, who wish to be whole, must forgive themselves and others.

23

This is the only way to free yourselves from your problems; there is no other.

No matter what is or was, by way of forgiveness you release yourselves from entanglement. This must take place via the heart, through love, for only then are you free.

Through this kind of release from old patterns of behaviour, you set others free and thus resolve the mental connections, the dependencies. Everyone can do this kind of release and forgiveness on their own.

You need not confront the other, freedom already comes through visualization/imagination. Each one can heal themselves in this way – quickly!

Those who forgive are at peace, and are cleansed from old patterns of conflict.

The relationships between men and women and also to children should change quickly.

Men of your era can only enter into the new energy once their behaviour towards women has been clarified. There is no difference because of sexuality, except sexuality.

Men and women are on the same level. The elevation of men in your society is bred. Women and men have equal rights at all levels. With this the oppression of women ends. This difference and the idea that women are second-class citizens existed in your minds only. In many cultures on planet Earth, women are put on the same level as serfs and domestic animals. Stop it!

We have talked about freedom and forgiveness, this is to be implemented with women worldwide as soon as possible. In this respect too, old patterns are to be resolved. Women and men are equal on all levels.

With God, all are equal: man and woman, woman and man.

Heed this, and live it.

Once this attitude changes, women will be treated equally in society. There will no longer be a difference in income and education. The relationship between men and women should be liberal and equal.

The children in your world should be treated equally and liberally too.

Children do not belong to their parents. They should only be cared for, supported and promoted during growth. Parents are responsible for their children, they should accept and live this. The souls of all children are more highly developed and more conscious than their parents; this has been planned deliberately. Your children are the creators of the 5th Dimension. They have brought this high level of awareness to Earth in order to live their task. As parents you should understand them, and attend them lovingly as they grow up, and supply them with everything a child needs. They do not need to be brought up because their consciousness teaches them. When children are not properly cared for, are restricted and pressurized, or treated unfairly, they immediately react with offensive conduct.

This is a signal for you as parents and serves to understand your child.

The energetic vibration of your children is higher than your own. As parents, educators and teachers, please take this into consideration.

Many parents can learn from their children. They are good teachers in forgiveness, ethics and morality, science and spirituality. Listen to your children when they talk to you, try to understand what they mean.

Be at peace with your family and laugh together. In harmony, this period of transformation can be coped with better. Enjoy your family, honour and appreciate them; these are your best learning fields. Do accept them.

The western and parts of the eastern world interact in forms of trading which you call economy. This type of exchange of goods has grown on the financial market. Worldwide trade is speculative and manipulative.

Change this into 'fair play', play honestly. Be truthful in trading too. There should be more transparency in these processes, within countries and globally. Large corporations often buy and sell at a loss thereby destroying the sales of small firms. This should be abandoned quickly. The monopoly of large companies harms every consumer. Your politicians are bribed and look on passively.

Citizens' money, tax money, too often flows and disappears into very dark channels. This obscure nature of the economy needs to be organized openly. Trade is important, the exchange of goods will continue, only the form needs to be discussed. Large companies which operate globally, need to be controlled by way of disclosing their transactions. Understanding this system will be beneficial to all.

The directors and consultants of companies and groups of companies should be honest and committed to their companies. Unfortunately, at present, the opposite applies.

Exaggerated salaries and payments prevent the neutral control of trade worldwide. This change is very sluggish, so be conscious of what you buy. Good consumer behaviour can support transparent, honest companies.

As the saying goes, 'the market regulates itself'. Thus manipulation and fraud will have no chance. Buy goods from companies which treat their employees fairly, and are honest and truthful in manufacture, sale and trade. Thus you will also improve this field.

The economic system too is changing. Big monopolies will be broken up. Extended transportation around the globe will be exposed as nonsensical and will no longer be needed. Mass turnover will change. Generally, less will be purchased. The new consciousness, the new human being, will still require goods as 'helpers'. These should have a good quality and durability.

That is the direction in which you are evolving, to the birth of a new world trade. Local products requiring short transportation will be preferred. The large artificial bubble of the economy will burst, and you will return to the simple way of trading with seasonal and local produce. This process of transformation will take several years, but will succeed with the help of politics. Once your politicians are genuine representatives of the citizens again, the economy will change - being forced to do so. Only a fair and transparent economy will endure in the 5th Dimension.

The switch to regional products will strengthen the regions allowing restructuring in the various regions. The cooperation and solidarity of the people in the various areas will change positively.

People living in the same area will see themselves as a unit again, and build a regional system of provision. This will enhance the individuality of the area and its inhabitants. Thus new honest trading systems will develop. The basic idea of trade will be practised, the excesses of the 3rd Dimension will disappear, and so the market will have cleansed itself.

To strengthen individuality, in all areas, is a pivotal point for the new era.

Do not confuse individuality with egoism. In the new era, egoism has no place. Egoism has led you to what you are living today.

Everyone cares for themselves, often to the detriment of others, unfortunately. This is what you practise in your family and world-wide too when dealing with states and nations. This behaviour will no longer be needed in the 5th Dimension. The new era will be brighter and lighter and will not allow these properties of low vibration.

Enrichment at the expense of others will no longer exist. More oneness and individuality are to be practised.

How is this to be understood?

Unity will enhance the sense of 'US'. Individuality is also needed to enhance oneness. Only those who are aware of their humanity with their individual strengths, can practise a strong feeling of "WE." This concerns everyone in the future. What strengthens the individual is self-confidence. Self-confidence is trained in your children within the family, schools, partnerships etc. Self-esteem without selfishness is the building block for oneness. You people can only be ethically and morally strong, if you are aware of your self-worth as human beings. Those who vibrate in harmony practise their natural self-confidence. A person's potential and charisma are indicative of their vibration. Harmonious, happy people are authentic and live their individual vital energy.

This specific, personal self-esteem has a high frequency and great strength.

Everyone should strive for this before thinking of unity, of 'US'. The various abilities of each one should be recognized, encouraged and considered good. Without presenting oneself or assuming a pose, everyone should just try their talents and abilities, and live these. Here the diversity of each one is required. Nothing but diversity strengthens oneness.

'WE', unity, cooperation must be based on equality.

In oneness, everyone is of equal value. There are no hierarchies in 'WE'; everyone is on the same level. This is your new form of society. The journey demands an ego-free strong sense of 'I'. Feelings and anxieties such as:

'I'm not good enough', or 'the other is better-looking than me' or 'I don't perform as expected', are inadequate for oneness. Therefore, each one of you should work on your own natural strength and harmony first. Those who vibrate in harmony, are not envious.

Feelings of aggression have no place in ego-free self-esteem. An important learning field for everyone is harmonious adaptation. Many of you are already involved in these learning processes. This includes overcoming anxiety and fear. Fear is always a lack of confidence. Trust the process of life, you are always divinely guided. Everything happens at the right time. Feel that you are guided, then so be it. In the depth of your heart, just trust. Once you have reached the new era, you will recognise the guidance and know that nothing happens without a reason. You are the creators of your lives, presently unconsciously, but consciously in the 5th Dimension. These are laborious steps which you have to take in order to free yourselves from your own patterns of belief. I beseech you to take this route, it is worth it; the knowledge, the awakening awaits you. Imagine that it is a kind of self-imposed test; thereafter, freedom awaits you. When this process has expanded your consciousness, you will understand all the interrelations.

Would this not be wonderful! The elevated light of the new era will lead you to freedom. All the shackles which you have imposed upon yourselves in many lives, you may now leave behind you. What really matters is the freedom for new opportunities of creation in all areas and on all levels. Please accept this challenge!

Strong, equal unity is important for the transformation of your life, for your society. Unity, 'WE', is composed of individual people with a good self-esteem. That is why it is so important for each of you to recognise that self-esteem must be natural and ego-free. There is no 'WE' if each one remains in their shell, 'Fear'. Recognise the importance of every human being, do not judge, do not condemn. Everyone, truly everyone, has their position to fill in the unit. People who live on the fringes of society, often have special talents. They too are needed, they too are to boost their self-esteem and to go into the new era. Assist one another in courses, seminars and lectures. Nurture your self-worth and cast off all doubts. You will succeed.

We from the spiritual realm know how difficult this process is for you. We support you with our powers so that you recognise and accept your self-worth. The egoism of your era is not needed in the new era. Egoism sows dependence, infatuation and strife; this has no place in the 5th Dimension.

Cast it off!

Liberal thoughts determine the phase of transformation. This is the only the way in which each one can raise their consciousness. Simply put your backpack of fears and old belief patterns aside. Turn towards it, say 'thank you', then peacefully forget everything you packed into it. For the new era, you need to be light and happy in order to live all your unexpected abilities.

Whether you are young, middle -aged or retired, each one is welcome in the 5th Dimension. Everyone has the opportunity to confidently participate in shaping the new Oneness. Even those who are sick should get moving. The bright light of the new era heals everything.

Have trust!

Your environment, which you call nature, is useful to you in the old as well as in the new era. It will be transformed by slight climatic changes. Some plants will leave the Earth and others will appear. Nature will take care of balancing the energies. Your energy can be recharged in nature. Walks, physical exercise, and simply being in the forest, meadow, or at the seaside strengthen your immune system and your body.

Nature is the home of fairies, elves, gnomes, dwarves, tree spirits, and many more. In the new era, these creatures will be visible to you and will offer means of communication. Their energy level is higher, and they direct and protect the plant world.

These creatures can be asked regarding the knowledge of plants. The world of nature spirits holds knowledge which, in botany and nutrition, provides new insight and deepens the understanding of plants, trees, insects and wild animals. It is a science which reveals itself by means of contact. The natural beings help to cleanse entire areas from pollution. Groundwater can be redirected and purified with their knowledge and assistance. Earth energies such as fractures and distortions in rock formations can be recognised and rectified with the help of the beings of nature. Take advantage of this opportunity to cleanse landscapes, rivers, soil and natural plants. This cleansing process heals the Earth.

Great changes will take place in the earth. They will occur slowly. You will recognise and avoid these areas. The earth cleanses itself from the inside. This cleansing comes to pass in a similar way your body cleanses itself. Water, lots of water will cleanse entire landscapes. Volcanic eruptions will cleanse the bowels of the earth. The wind will cleanse the etherial body of the earth. These cleansing processes of the earth are slowly being set into motion now and are to be respected. The Earth, Gaia, is a large living being with a very high level of consciousness. This consciousness has already reached the 5th Dimension. Therefore Gaia's cleansing processes are so vital, as are your own.

The rivers wish to assume their natural courses again, so respect and support them in so doing. Each body of water on Earth has a consciousness and thus should be treated with respect. When building near the sea and along rivers, remember the great power of water and hence the intelligence of these Beings. In many areas on Earth, the sea will wish to expand itself. During full moon phases, take note of the power and intelligence of your oceans. Respect and accept this power. Among you there will be people who recognise the consciousness of the earth, the rivers and the oceans. They will and ought to try to calm and direct the forces of these Beings. Accept the changes of Gaia, they are cleansing processes for the benefit of all beings on and in the earth. They are already at work and are inevitable.

You should refrain from using nuclear energy. Nuclear fission is a natural process. You have made it into the destructive force the atom now has. Peaceful uses are possible and do not leave any nuclear waste. The earth itself will resolve the nuclear contamination. The deposits will be neutralised by water and gas. The spiritual world will support these processes so that they can be completed quickly. Within a short time, clarifying bacteria will allow light energy into the contaminated areas again.

The climatic changes of the Earth are already underway. Slowly, the climate is changing. In a few years, strong solar winds will reach the earth. Reddish lights in the sky will herald the oncoming solar winds. Among you there will be people who work with the elements. They will moderate these hot winds. The solar winds clarify the ether layer around the Earth. This may sound fantastic, but let it be said that these processes are already at work and on their way to you. People with medial abilities and the knowledge of what is needed, will be able to calm and direct the elements somewhat. The spiritual world trains and works with these people. When the time of implementation has come, they will be ready and will accept their task. Just trust!

Many readers among you will suggest that St. Germain is being very fanciful. But be sure, this will be your reality. Prepare yourselves for these changes, and you will not be taken by surprise. At the right time, each person will be exactly where they are needed. Trust divine guidance!

What is trust? Why am I talking of trust?

Trust is an acceptance of reliability at a spiritual level. This attitude calms your nervous system on an energetic level. It is not a simple reassurance 'all is well'. In the spiritual area of your body, this energy of trust gives you the confidence that everything will turn out according to a plan the mind has no access to. Trust lovingly switches your mind off. Your mind receives the message 'This is not your responsibility'. When trusting yourself or other people, you automatically adapt to a higher energy. Trust helps, for example, to heal your body and to resolve conflicts. Trust is the energy the 5th Dimension is made up from. It is a high light energy which you only encounter sometimes, but which is sensed as love, peace, and harmony at a deep level. In your books of God it is often equated with faith. 'To believe in something' can be understood as 'having trust in something'. Energetically, faith in God and trust in God is an equally high light energy. The energy of God is the highest energy you can achieve on Earth. In the new era you will not only feel this energy but will consciously recognise it. The all-encompassing, infinitely loving light energy upholds your universe, your Earth and yourselves. In the 5th Dimension, the frequency of this light or divine energy is only slightly increased. Your body cannot easily cope with this energy boost and must therefore be slowly adjusted. These adjustments take place by clarifying, refining and purifying at all levels of the aura as well as the body. You need this phase of transition. If you want to train yourselves energetically, then practise this through trust.

First trust in yourself. Let trust be the basis of your thoughts, actions, desires and ideas. In so doing you increase your energy field and positively change your aura. The second step is to trust other people or situations. To trust another is an energetic closeness which you allow consciously. You let go of controlling your mind and rely on another person or situation: 'all will be well'. This deep trust resonates in all your cells and imparts serenity. You need this serenity to live life creatively. The mind needs creativity to be occupied. The body needs to be occupied to stay active and healthy. Thus you recognise the meaning of life. Trust is the foundation all actions are based on. Therefore, practise trusting yourself and others. Trust boosts self-confidence, and everyone needs this too. Do you now understand the importance of trust? Trust elevates your energy system, easily and quickly.

When a person has achieved a high level of energy, i.e. light energy, and lives accordingly, life is easier. Blockages, which prevent realization, are of a lower frequency and block all projects. Progress is not possible because energy flows too slowly along the pathways, stagnates or is blocked entirely. When somebody runs on high frequencies, on light energy, everything happens without hindrance, runs quietly and smoothly. This is desirable. The success of many projects is enhanced by high frequencies of light. This applies to you as well, you remain calmer, more focused, and thus your project develops more successfully than if you approach tasks in a nervous and hectic way. Blockages are resolved by high frequencies of energy. Trust allows these high energies to flow into your systems.

'Trust first yourself, your actions, your thoughts and your deeds.'

Train yourself daily in this energy increase by simply trusting, trusting yourself. If you succeed in this, you can apply it to everything else in your life.

For a long time there have been UFO sightings worldwide. Many people do not believe to have seen a UFO (unidentified flying object) and find many rational excuses. You accept having seen all sorts of things, but no UFOs. In many countries on Earth energy gates have been opened by the spiritual world; there the veil has been removed from the Earth's ether layer. So it is possible, within these energy gates, to see UFOs and even various other non-terrestrial phenomena. They are real. Presently your Earth is being visited by many Beings for study purposes. Many other forms of life are curious about your ascent from dense matter into the 5th Dimension.

It is very instructive for other beings to observe you. Some of the beings from other galaxies enter via the light gates of Earth, others visit you via the universe's magnetic radiation, which upholds and aligns your planet.

Starting from points in the sun, these magnetic rays, which are invisible, penetrate the Earth. It is thus held in position, lightly floating. By beings from other planets these magnetic rays can be used as energy ladders, as an entrance and exit to and from the Earth.

You are visited by many scholars and other interested parties with very positive intentions. They usually come in groups and are invisible to you due to their high frequency. They show themselves to few people, and communication which you call telepathy takes place. They readily provide information concerning their missions, and are joyful, loving beings.

The meaning of life is to attain the realization of who you really are. Here on Earth you humans are trapped in a body. Your true form is a spark of light, your soul. At birth this spark of light entered the body and considers the human body its home. Using this body, the soul can operate on Earth. The body has the molecular density to live, learn, and work on Earth. The soul's experiences are stored as feelings in the physical cells. All experiences, spiritual as well as physical, are stored via the mental level, as feelings. Your feelings tell you if something was good or less so for your soul. Pain, too, is a feeling that has settled in the body, in the cells. Pain is an indication that something is not good for the soul. When the body experiences pain, the 'alarm', as you call it, goes off. Then you should look and listen to what the pain is telling you. Pain always indicates deficits at the soul level. Pain is a good sign for you to go within, to question yourselves, and to change your circumstances, your attitudes, your intentions, and much more.

Pain induces you to wake up, the soul, the body. This only happens subconsciously. The subconscious mind is the hub of the soul. Now it is up to you to raise the problem from the subconscious, to look at yourselves and bring about change. This is how your learning processes on Earth take place. The soul incarnates, assumes a human body in order to learn, to achieve completion and accomplishment. Again and again, through many lifetimes your soul dwells on Earth, in various cultures and eras. Sometimes you are good persons with lessons to learn, sometimes you are less good with corresponding lessons to be learnt. The only aim is for your soul to reach perfection, to experience all the wisdom the material world of Earth holds in store. Time, how often you incarnate, does not matter. This depends on the individual.

Once the soul has recognised the wisdom of the Earth, you will enter into a new, a higher vibration, and will live there, in whatever form. Each planet has its own areas of learning. Your soul is the true *You*, that which endures for ever.

The soul is eternal.

The spark of light, the soul, strives for perfection on Earth, and universally too. The goal is to become one with omnipotence, which you call God, or the Central Sun, or Nirvana or … . There are many names for *the Great One, the All That Is.*

The situations through which you live in many lives shape you into what you are.

In meditation you can look into past lives and recognise the meaning: the why? Sometimes it helps to take a review in order to understand why in this life time one repeatedly encounters this or that. The understanding gained through observation during a particular meditation may also be helpful in identifying the reasons for disease or a recurring thought pattern. Use this kind of viewing to train yourself, to recognise yourself and also to accept as truth what you have seen. The truth is that you have all lived on Earth as human beings, many times.

How then can death be explained? How can you understand the death of a human being?

Birth is the entrance into human life, so death, the act of dying, is the exit. There are many ways of dying. Everybody chooses their own way. Each one dies according to their disposition. Do not compare ways of dying; it will not make sense to fathom why this or the other person departed from the Earth differently. Even every birth is different. Birth and death often show the individuality of a soul. For everything there is a reason and it is difficult for you to explain logically. When somebody leaves this world, it is always their own decision. They have chosen to do it exactly that way and not differently. Neither the will nor the intellect has made this choice. No, it is the subconscious mind on behalf of the soul that has determined this. The soul decides when to leave the body. People often suspect that their time of departure has come. The body often senses the weakness before the spark of life extinguishes. Many people even die consciously because they are aware of their soul plan, or because they wish to start anew as a human being, in a new body. There are many reasons as to why a person dies in a certain way and not differently.

In many cultures, the subject of death is viewed with fear. None of you wants to know when you or a relative will leave this world. It is connected with parting, finally letting go, and releasing. What you love, you hate to let go of, voluntarily.

This is why you often hold on to people for a long time even after they have died. Have trust, death is a natural process in the life of every human being. Give the deceased freedom by keeping their memory in your heart, but set them free in your consciousness, in your mind. Only thus can the soul go *home*, return to its energy home. We in the spiritual world say a soul ascends into the light and goes home. This soul does not disappear; in the light spheres, it undergoes a learning process and meets all the others who preceded it.

When the time has come according to the soul's own plan, each soul decides to re-incarnate and to be born to live a new life. Such is your life cycle. Death is to be seen as the end of an option. At soul level, you will meet and recognise each other again.

In the soul's plan, getting lost is not possible. Therefore, understanding what death is, you should not cling to the grief of this experience. Suffering is a selfish feeling at the emotional level. Suffering means, I refuse to let go. For this reason, I ask you to consciously open yourself when approaching a dying person, and also in regard to your own death as well as that of friends and family members. Please respect each individual's decision according to their soul plan.

Let go of the departed souls, so that they can ascend into the light and be free. Keep them in loving memory, but do not hold on to them through *grief.* Souls who are hindered from ascending remain earthbound. They remain in the homes as sparks of light, or cling to people they were very fond of. Being earthbound is very difficult and painful for a soul. In the earthbound condition, a spark of light cannot realise its intended soul plan.

Often, the soul remains with the family because it thinks it can still offer comfort or make a difference. In this state it is hardly possible, except with great effort and sacrifice. This often happens when there are unsolved conflicts in the family, or when souls do not know about ascension and do not trust the Light. These are difficult situations and they can only be settled with great effort. In the years to come, more people will become aware of these things and be able to help in the ascension of these earthbound souls. This topic should be dealt with openly so that everyone is aware of the meaning of death. Please realise the real processes of dying because if you understand them, you can deal with them with greater freedom and openness.

I Am St. Germain, and, with divine love, I support you in your processes of learning and transformation.

The spiritual Christ, Sananda, revives the energy of Christ

The I Am-Presence of the Spiritual Christ speaks to you, and reveals all that was hidden in the past.
I am the presence of Sananda, your Christ in spirit.

My messages help you to understand how the Christ energy works with you, at present as well as in the elevated frequency, which you call the 5th Dimension.

The image you have of Christ has deliberately been falsified. The way in which the world views Christ and God was meant to generate dependency and anxiety. Consequently, power games of the churches arose quickly. Your churches today all still have these power structures. You are beginning to realise this. By recognising this immense manipulation you can change your attitude to these institutions.

Many people are withdrawing from the church, unfortunately for base motives, just to save money. For a long time already, for some of you, the church has not offered a place where you feel mentally at home. You are disappointed by the way the church operates, and you find no answers to your questions. The church is still dominated by rituals: baptism, church services, feasts, celebrations, and funerals. These rituals are often loveless acts. The church as shaper of society with ethical and moral demands no longer exists. The interpretations of biblical scriptures, of the Qur'an, and others differ vastly, often lacking the essential energy inherent in the original scripture.

These changes regarding institutions of worship and religious groups are always man-made. Jesus Christ and God the Father have not changed; their energy is eternal and operates in the light, eternally. The betrayal of the divine energy took place during the religious wars, and is still current in the ignorant, misleading interpretation of the scriptures. Trust, faith, is lacking.

The church and other institutions of worship lack the intellectual depth of wisdom. The scriptures of the Bible, the Qur'an, and others are partially still pure divine energy. But also parts of the scriptures were consciously and unconsciously distorted to spread fear among mankind.

Fear is the best dependency game played on your Earth. Former spiritual leaders understood and implemented this very well, to the alleged 'well-being' of institutions of worship.

This was and still is the abuse of power in the name of my Father, God.

These machinations of abuse will soon be revealed by the energies of transparency, which are reaching your Earth.

Your monarchs and politicians have almost always been allies of religious institutions, and in earlier times were determined by them. This era of powerful churches, mosques, etc. is changing due to your increased consciousness. The way religious institutions are now organised cannot prevail.

The liberal, fair, and divine thought of wisdom is to enter into the systems and to serve as a catalyst for change. The collapse of the old structures is sealed.

The son of God, Jesus Christ, reveals his secret and hereby corrects what has deliberately been falsely presented for thousands of years.

Now the time has come to rewrite the life of Jesus and of the people of your world.

The one who is known to you from your books as Jesus Christ, is light energy sent by God the father. This light energy was pure consciousness in the spirit God the Father. With his life Jesus Christ paved the way for the new age.

The scriptures of the various books of faith were written and often changed. This was the onset of the ethical transformation of the energies, which, at the time, were very low on Earth. Jesus Christ was truly sent by God the Father, and at death became one with the energy of God the Father again. The death of Jesus shows you the Resurrection in the Light. The body and soul of Jesus ascended into the Divine Light. This presentation shows you how the ascension into the Light, this "coming home", takes place. Although these passages in the Bible were changed, the core 'ascension into heaven' remained.

Just trust, the dying process of every soul takes place in the same way. The body remains on Earth; it is physical and is returned to the Earth, the great soul of Gaia.

It is a sign of gratitude for providing the physical vehicle. When departing you return it, even though it is worn out. The great soul takes it back again, regardless whether as ashes or a body. It returns to the physical cycle of life.

The ascent of the soul into heaven, into the light, is beneficial and important for you.

The life cycle of every human being concludes with the ascent into the spheres of light.

An earthbound soul clogs the etherial body of the Earth, and Gaia is unable to breathe properly. Imagine the etherial body surrounding the Earth as an enormous filter. It reaches 40.000 metres into the sky and spans the entire planet. This layer acts as a filter for your Earth.

When a filter is clogged, it cannot fulfil its task, as you well know. It no longer works.

Due to the numerous wars and due to ignorance, many souls wander around in the etherial body of the Earth and clog it. The cleansing process is to begin now so that Gaia can breathe again and can actively work on the ascent into the new energy. The etherial body of the Earth is being cleansed.

This cleansing process is prepared on a spiritual level and people support it. The consciousness of a person able to do this work needs to be awake.

Some people are already active in the service of the spiritual world, have knowledge of the etherial body of the Earth, and know how to release earthbound souls into the light by setting up columns of light. This is a great service to Gaia and to the earthbound souls. Many souls do not know how to ascend. In your culture, there are no instructions and no help given. The churches have no answers nor instructions regarding ascension into the light.

Light columns are elevators of ascension to the home dimension of the soul.

When a soul goes 'home', it can help by releasing energy, in order to render a valuable service to the family members. In the spheres of light, the soul is still able to direct and steer things for those left on Earth. However, if the soul remains earthbound, it requires great effort and it is difficult to succeed in its efforts. Souls who remain earthbound, still experience pain and pressure, and may suffer. Should the soul decide to remain in the earthly realm, close to family members, its development stagnates. Many earthbound souls also believe they are still alive, they have not realised their death.

During the process of dying, the dying person sees the light weeks, days, or hours before death. The soul recognizes the path of light, and is often met by souls of deceased persons or animals. This is a joyful reunion. Ignorance of this separation process, sudden accidental death or great suffering of relatives causes many souls to remain earthbound, without a body. The spark of light (soul) wanders around trying to resolve situations.

Those who depart in peace and who are prepared, who decide to leave, can ascend through the channel of light. The strong presence of light, the Elohim energies, which are very loving and affectionate, gently escort the soul. When consciousness on Earth increases, these angels will be visible to many people. This reassures the relatives enabling them to let the person die in peace. For the relatives this is an act of peace and letting go. Being reassured, they can allow things to take their course, and take leave.

Ancient cultures were aware of these processes, accepted and celebrated them. You people today are often uninformed and can therefore not understand what is happening. This is to change now. I am Sananda. I help you to understand, and lead you.

The process of birth of a human being is identical, just the other way round. The soul leaves its home and travels through the light channel into the human body on Earth. This departure from home is a letting-go. With incarnation - as the ritual of rebirth is called - a new field of learning or adventure begins for the soul.

It is a perpetual cycle until the final incarnation and a conscious dying. Then the mature soul, often the enlightened soul, enters a higher energy. The learning process on Earth is then complete. A conscious person, who is aware of these processes, dies in acceptance and peace.

I Am the spiritual Christ, Sananda, and guide you so you can understand.

Those who burden themselves with guilt by lying, cheating or manipulating others incriminate their own development. They become involved in an illusion. The seductions of your present world are all built on fraud and manipulation. They are often difficult to recognise. The truth, if you are really seeking, is to be found in your heart. Your heart makes itself felt via your feelings. If you sense 'something is not quite right here', follow this and trust your intuition. In your present world, it is hard not to give in to temptations. Pay attention to yourselves, to your feeling, and remain in the truth.

Truth is the simplest path, it is the easiest to follow.

Should you leave the path of truth and follow temptation, you will follow the hard way with many obstacles. You will follow the material world with its many excesses of money and power. Those who give in to the entanglement of temptation are captured by these energies and a disentanglement from the circumstances of lying, cheating, and manipulation is very slow and tedious.

Often a long ordeal ensues, which stretches across more than one lifetime. These excesses can only be rectified with knowledge and courage, for it takes a lot of courage to ascend from the inferior, lower energies.

This change is easiest effected by forgiving yourself and making amends with all victims. Forgiveness, forgiving yourself and others, is the way out of all entanglements. This is a hard road to take, but with knowledge and understanding it leads to freedom. The freedom of heart, the soul in a free body, is the ideal state to live creatively. Those who are guilty are not free.

Your thoughts, your conscience, is constantly tied up with this topic, even though you may be able to suppress it for a certain time. It dominates your system.

The universal law decrees: those who burden themselves with guilt, cause karma for their souls. Negative karma is the universal term for guilt. According to the spiritual law, this karma has to be redeemed. There are many ways of doing this because there are countless possibilities of clearing situations.

The first step is to forgive oneself in order to be released from guilt. Thereafter, in your material world, there are many solutions for the next steps, which depend on the topic, and match the temperament of a person.

The guilt you have inflicted on others hits you hardest. You are burdened, feel guilty, and your actions are hampered.

Karma (guilty feelings) will not exist in the 5th Dimension. The high presence of light will immediately recognize low motives and will transform thoughts of 'guilt'. Immediately!

The light and frequency in the 5th Dimension will instantly uncover lower energies, and thus a topic can be dealt with and released immediately. Practise purifying yourselves now already and try to recognise 'temptation' with the help of your feelings. Only with the help of your mental attitude will you be able to dwell on the right path, leading to freedom. Your only duty is towards yourself, towards your soul plan. That does not mean allowing your selfishness to run wild, adopting the attitude 'Make way, here I come'. This implies transferring the responsibility you have for yourselves to other people as well. Treat people, animals, and plants the way you would like to be treated. This is a sign of a heightened degree of responsibility towards yourself and others. Would such behaviour not be ideal - simply heavenly!

If your conscience is clear, and you understand and are aware of your personal responsibility, you already find yourself in the 5th Dimension. This is the result of your conscious thought and action. This is how easy the ascent into the high energy takes place.

The spiritual world is pleased to help you in all processes of recognition, and guides you with love. Ask for guidance and support from the spiritual world, and you will receive it. Simply asking will do the trick!

There are spirit guides, angels, archangels, ascended masters, many deities, and also the world of nature with its fairies, unicorns, gnomes, and many other beings willing to help you in learning, or who will teach you. It is possible to talk to your spirit guides, to contact them. The spirit guides are waiting to be asked so they may finally respond to you.

Be still and meditate, ask your questions and remain still expecting the answers. This requires exercise, so be patient.

The veil between the spiritual and material worlds has never been this diaphanous. It is now possible to be mentally guided into the new energy (World).

Trust the answers. The spirit guides have only your best interests at heart. They love you so deeply and are only too willing to train you. We from the spiritual world have all come to assist in the ascension of the Earth into the higher sphere. Simply out of love.

It is meant to be a great success, and we wish to take along all embodied souls. All people are to participate in the change. This is the will of God!

This project has been planned for a long time. With love, we are all looking forward to it.

The new, high energies which flow to the Earth affect your appearance. Today you believe in the statement that cells have to grow old, so the body ages. Your appearance is aging with the increasing number of years. This belief system has been shaped over the millennia and is part of being human. The aging of the body is the ideal way to leave the used body, to die. This is the way it has always been to date.

This may change, now!

Due to the increased energy of the Earth, the aging process of cells and thus the body will be stopped. It will now be possible for all of you to slow down the aging process, and even stop it. This understanding stems from the altered consciousness. You believe that you are aging. Well, your cells, your body, are doing what you think. Your thoughts shape your reality. What you think happens, it is your truth. If you were to think differently, the truth would change around and within you. Thinking influences your body and your outer reality. Your thinking shapes your world, inside and out. What you think is reflected on the outside, your physical body, i.e. your appearance. Be aware of how powerful your thoughts are. When you think 'red', the traffic light turns red and slows you down. When you think 'green', the light turns green and offers you free passage. This is just one example of how thinking shapes reality. It is meant to show you clearly that you can slow yourselves down mentally or allow yourselves to continue unhindered. This can be applied to the cells, the body.

If you believe in the aging process, the wrinkles will appear on your face. If, however, you believe in the youthful freshness and dynamics of your cells, your body, this will take place.

In the 3rd Dimension, in which the Earth still partially finds itself, the process of life is seen as birth - youth - middle age - old age - death.

This can now be changed.

The light energy of the Earth no longer makes aging inevitable. Of course, you may choose to age but it is no longer necessary. Thanks to the high energy you now have the opportunity to think 'eternal youth and dynamics'. By so doing you re-programme your cells, and it happens. The high frequency allows for this kind of youthful aging. This is part of the new design diversity of possibilities.

Have fun with it, try it out, it works.

In this way you switch off the old belief patterns of 'age', 'growing old', and the associated problems.

What do you now think about retirement homes? People with a long life span on Earth no longer need to try out the experience of old age. Of course it will still be allowed, you may still age, if you wish to try it out. It is just not necessary any more. You may consciously retain your cells in a fresh and youthful state and you do not need to experience an aging body.

This is a great social change.

Thus, many things will be possible in the future, through the new way of conscious thinking.

People who live on Earth for many years will gain lots of experience and will be highly respected and esteemed scholars for the younger generation. They will be required to teach and train. They will be respected because, in spite of many years of life, they will have retained the freshness and vitality inwardly and outwardly.

Truly, a new era begins.

Please try the new way of thinking and see what it does to the cells and the body. Try it out.

The wisdom of humanity is about to experience a breakthrough. You will be able to access the ancient knowledge from your cells and earlier cultures. Due to the high frequency of light, it will be available to those who are interested. You people extend yourselves though the activation of your chakras, the energy vortices in the aura field around the body. These energy wheels are opened and activated by the irradiating energy. This results in a higher energy level. Physically you perceive that your perceptions are stronger and clearer. This clarity brings about a clearing in relationships and life circumstances. For each of you, this results in a better self-awareness and a sensing of what is right and wrong. Have the courage to confront these experiences and to accept them. This clearing process is what you need to become more aware. This process allows lots of light energy to flow into the systems of the body, thus expanding consciousness. The perception of yourselves is more differentiated. You sense when something is wrong with you, when something is not harmonious in and around you. The ability to sense makes you question, and then to detect the interference and change it. A salutary refining and cleansing process of the body and the auric field. The aura is your personal energy field around the body. This energy field has been installed to protect and strengthen the body.

You were born with the four denser layers of the aura. The energy field, the aura, is a definite part of the human body. Clairvoyant people recognise the aura, they can see it. Jesus radiated a bright and clear, an extended aura. Due to His strong, bright aura, He attracted people and was therefore perceived as a special being.

In the aura, below the feet and above the head, there are two chakras, which, in the ensuing years, will be activated in many people by irradiation. The chakras below the feet are called 'Earth star' and above the head 'Star-gate'. When these gates are opened, each individual has access to the wisdom of their previous lives. This state of development is required for ascent into the 5th Dimension. In those in whom all chakra gates have been opened, inner peace will occur along with the feeling of freedom. A major creative force and clarity will be perceived. We from the spiritual world wish this process upon everyone, for then the new age can begin.

With the help of God I lovingly brought these truths to you.
The spiritual energy of Christ, Sananda

Kuthumi explains the expansion of consciousness

I am Master Kuthumi. I direct the golden ray of light.
My messages are to help you expand your consciousness in order to
aid your progress into the new energy. I rejoice with you!

Great changes await planet Earth. You need to trust that everything happens at the right time as it has been predetermined. At this time everyone will experience an expansion in consciousness, whether they want it or not. You cannot shield yourselves from the light energy, it penetrates you. Your cells, your entire body will be cleansed, you cannot stop this consciously.

Your mind will become more sensitive, and this too must be accepted by the systems in your body.

Please accept the vibrations of light, and rejoice. Enlighten yourselves! Seek information concerning these processes, so you will understand and go through them faster. Mental acceptance accelerates the change in your body, and there will be no strong effects (cramps) in muscle and nerve tissues. Should you resist, this will result in extreme tension in the muscle tissue and in electrolytic disturbances in the nervous system. The flooding of your body with light will not be pain free.

Accept the processes and be prepared. Pressure in the head are waves of vibration wishing to penetrate the cells and thereby the body. It can be said that these are signals of entry. Thus you can feel the vibrations of light. Should you oppose these indispensable waves which want to change your body, you will experience pain and your nervous system will collapse. This is felt as pain in the arms and legs, and also the back and shoulder areas may be affected. High pressure on one or both temples is normal.

Now you know what awaits you, accept it, and the pain will subside.

The density of your body is to be enlightened; it is a highly energetic process, which does not simply happen overnight while sleeping. It demands a transformative process which extends over a longer period of time. Do not give in to fear and think you are ill; it is the adaptation to the new light on Earth. Be patient with your body and withdraw from activities for a while.

Remain calm, your nervous system will be grateful. Light work and exercise will counteract the stress. If your nerves are overstimulated by too much activity, this may lead to collapse. Take longer breaks during the day and go out into nature. This relaxes the nerves. The nervous system can be calmed by eating fruit daily, for fructose calms the nerves. Drinking lots of water (boiled if possible) flushes all toxins from the body quickly and helps the nerves to normalize their frequencies.

By accepting these changes, you counteract blockages, pressure and pain.

Accept the change, it is inevitable. It affects people of all ages.

Your animals, especially pets, pass through this renewal period very quickly because they feel what is happening and are filled with joy and hope. For love of their owners, animals often take the pressure upon themselves, and inexplicable illnesses come to the fore. Do understand this and accept your responsibility. The pressure on the animal can be cured by love and lots of attention.

Accepting responsibility is not a novel idea of the light frequency. To accept responsibility for oneself, for one's thoughts, deeds and actions, is necessary, and allows one to 'mature', to 'grow'.

This is what you now need most: the realization that you are responsible for yourself. None but yourself!

The light waves from the universe reach Earth continuously and are well regulated.

This is sensed by the brightness of the light. Your light, the sun, shines brighter. The air, the ether, is enriched with lots of light molecules. After a walk in nature you feel tired. Light molecules are fed into your system. This process is quite normal, accept it and rejoice. An increased radiation of light reached Earth in December 2012. This bright wave of light reached all those who lived on Earth then and are still alive today.

More waves with photons will reach Earth periodically; this will continue for a number of years. Look forward to how these waves of light will gradually change lots of things. Firstly yourself, your body. Energetic disturbances may or may not occur. Due to the light, you will be thirstier; accept this. Your body will automatically reduce your food intake; this too should be regarded as normal.

The high irradiation nourishes your cells. Be not concerned, everything has been planned and prepared for, and has thus been determined by the universe and God the Father (always including God the Mother).

After this extended exposure, your body will feel lighter and more relaxed, so look forward to it. Your thought processes, too, will change. Your thoughts may seem strange to you, this is normal. Your thoughts will be lighter, clearer and purer.

During the change, an inner serenity is desirable and helpful.

It has been decided that further light waves will reach the Earth in the ensuing years. The waves will increase exponentially and their intensity will rise continually.

Your society is composed of various social structures.

There are families, singles, couples who live together as husband and wife or as man and man or woman and woman, home-sharing communities, and separate families. Many living possibilities have been created and accepted over the years, always with the prospect of more liberality in everyday life; and looking at it, it is liberal. Everyone has the opportunity to choose their way of life.

Often, however, groups of suffering people, or people with the same or similar social and educational backgrounds form a community.

In the case of such a social choice, a potentiated connection comes about. The areas of learning which need to be addressed are attracted more promptly. The areas of learning, problems as you call them, are increased. These communities often fail because of the increased power of attraction. The community is burdened with too many problems and difficulties. In most cases, clarification seems hopeless. Thus, this way of life is doomed to fail.

Therefore, be more mindful of the way of life you choose and prepare yourselves for the learning process. In relationships a lot of karma (accumulated debt from past lives) can be worked through and cleansed. This is the only way freedom can be attained.

Unsolved circumstances arise when communities part aggressively or emotionally.

If issues have not been resolved, problems are amplified in the ensuing social structure, and ignoring and evading them becomes inevitable. Then you must either confront the problem or leave the community once more. And so it goes on and on. Every unsolved learning situation is amplified in the future.

After many marriages, for example, many people maintain that the first marriage was the best, 'If only I had changed this or that'.

This is the realization: When I run away from a problem, it confronts me again and again, but more pronounced. When you realise that running away, looking the other way, or avoiding and ignoring change only exacerbates the issue - tackle your conflicts and problems, deal with them!

The clarification of learning areas is your only path to freedom.

Social structures are the most emotional learning areas of life.

Occupational areas are also good for learning, be they emotional or intellectual.

Be aware of this, if you seek to change your field of occupation.

First clear your relationships in the old company (for example) before you apply to another. Do not change because you cannot stand something, but because you are interested in new areas of learning, new challenges. A change is always rewarding, but from an aspect of freedom. As the saying goes, 'one rises to the occasion', and this is true!

Spiritual growth is to be sought after, because it results in development at all levels.

The elimination of karma or guilt (although there is no such thing as guilt) is a process of clarification, without which you cannot proceed into the new energy. The so-called guilt is just a term I choose to illustrate that it is a perpetration extending across many lives. Guilt per se is non-existent in the universe. You on Earth use this term. What is meant is that the soul wishes to correct mistakes made in this and in previous lives. This option is absolutely self-imposed by each soul because no other can interfere in the soul plan of another.

The only exceptions regard spirit guides and angels. With permission from the soul, they may undertake restructuring from the spiritual world.

The issues of guilt, revenge, hatred, and resentment are basic energies, which are solely earthbound.

Your religions have created a dependency around these issues in order to manipulate you more effectively. To God the Father and God the Mother guilt or anything similar are non-existent.

The divine energy is almighty and unimaginably pure and light. Basic attachments such as guilt cannot reach these high frequencies of light. To the universe the belief that one has to justify oneself to God and expect punishment is unknown. One can only justify towards oneself.

Where one's conscience is concerned, every individual is answerable solely to themselves. Please accept this message; take it to heart.

By taking responsibility for your actions, thoughts and deeds you get out of the rut of karma, and no new karma is created.

Through this process of clarification you reach freedom.

Your own freedom!

Leave all dependencies of guilt behind you.

I would like to enlighten you about selfishness.

What is selfishness?

In your society, selfish behaviour is registered and accepted. That this behaviour is socially unacceptable, is well-known. In children and adolescents you still try to prevent and reverse this selfish behaviour, through education. In adults it is often tolerated, and even accepted. When it comes to profit margins in banking, financial markets and business in general, selfishness is prominent and is regarded as good business acumen.

This behavioural pattern should be recognised and reconsidered.

Selfishness is obsolete. For the new era it is no longer needed.

Selfishness is not good for world economy nor for the individual. It puts you under pressure. All body systems are burdened with congestion. On the economic market, pressure triggers stress and possibly a collapse, i.e. a standstill. Recognise selfishness for what it is: the means to power and greed.

It is not easy to track down selfishness.

It is found in the human system, but where?

Selfishness was created as a warning signal. In case of danger, it was to warn and attract attention so that one could defend oneself and avert danger. Thus, selfishness is very active and alive in the body. It even deserves praise for the good job it does, which is vitally important. A good activity for the ego.

Since you often live very civilized lives and danger is not constantly threatening you, the ego is bored. It has sought a new field of action. It puts the body under pressure. By doing this, it wants mankind to live more actively. Thus it would have more to do. Greater activity often ends up in the realm of will, and thus greed and power have been generated unconsciously. It is a very complicated process, which is difficult to fathom. Who searches after their ego in the body? It is not easy to find. In the body, the ego has no specific seat. In every individual, the ego energy occupies a different location, namely where pain or pressure is experienced. There the ego's point of action can often be located.

In meditation, by consciously making contact and by calling the ego, it can be tracked down and calmed. Often it is willing to move into the heart, where you ought to lovingly accommodate it. There it will possibly busy itself with something new.

Of course, it should retain its activity as warning signal, and this you should be grateful for.

By loving acceptance and some control by your consciousness, the ego becomes quieter and gentler. You must not banish it from your system because it warns you - that is its job. It should restrict itself to this, and you respect it for so doing.

An overwrought ego can also continuously mobilize fear.

Chemical substances in the body indicate *danger*, and fear arises. Fear usually refrains from daring actions, which is what fear is there for. However, when the body is constantly in a state of fear, self- confidence is impaired, and one speaks of a 'fearful person'. Thus the ego is *too* active.

Here, too, understanding the processes, and the loving acceptance of the ego are recommended, along with the request to concentrate on its actual job. Some control is advisable!

How does the ego appear within the system of power and greed?

Many people who have the same patterns of behaviour are drawn together, and this results in competition. Here egoism is needed. It recognises its duty. It constantly warns and adds fuel to the fire. A spiral is set in motion, which is hard to stop. Everyone wants more, wants to be better than the other, and the ego rejoices. It is very busy operating the warning system.

Thus the egoistic behaviour on the financial market arises.

These metaphors are transferable to all areas of your societies.

Do you understand how the ego operates?

Please limit it using your expanded consciousness and accept it fondly.

It will calm down, and the physical pressure will decrease.

Selfishness and the ego have a clear role to play in your body and should be limited to this.

If everyone can control this, society and the economic systems will develop freely and fairly. Fair, honest conditions in the market place will change the picture of the economy on Earth. The process of change begins with each individual. Each one has to limit their ego lovingly and remind it of its natural duty. Your human mind controls your ego and thus the system of power and greed is pacified.

Your ethical and moral principles have shaped many cultures on Earth and are nevertheless similar, almost identical. Ethics means spiritual and physical purity. Light at every level. On Earth, the purity of mankind in thought and deed has always been a law of great strength and truthfulness. The current world society has departed from this path and now lives by the rules of power. Many discussions and negotiations worldwide are highly manipulated and led by heads of state. Today, as in the past, allies are sought in order to act together against other countries. Ethics, clarity, and purity are not the supreme principles.

In order to convert society into the new era, ethics is now a criterion which should be sought after, worldwide. The moral excesses of your society should be cleansed as soon as possible. In many schools, the subject 'ethics' is taught. Children and adolescents are supposed to lay the foundations of their lives and become aware of their behaviour.

This is a good path to follow.

Previously, religion assumed the ethical teaching. Today, the concept of religion often does not fit into modern society. Role models, idols in an ethical sense are hard to find because the media immediately uncover motives or misconduct.

Who is to set the guiding principle in the area of ethics? Every individual must find this out for themselves.

The experience and circumstances of an individual play an important role. Parents, grandparents and friends can give guidance. Even the media play a part in the game of ethics, of course with different roles.

How are these factors to be considered and classified?

The influences of the Middle Ages, the age of barbarians, where the stronger fought their way with the sword, are over.

Unfortunately, time has stood still for many countries in Africa and a few in South America. Here too we hope for speedy clarification by the rise in consciousness on your planet.

The cornerstones of ethical life orientation are enshrined in your laws. The killing of people is illegal. Disregard of property is punishable. Physical conflicts are violations of peaceful communication. So, the cornerstones are there.

Every person is responsible for their actions! This is a prerequisite for a mature citizen.

For the new transparent light energy not only the cornerstone of this ethical orientation is required. Everyone should define their ethical goals themselves. It would be worthwhile for mankind to orient themselves on a high level of individual responsibility – individually and yet unified.

This is what it could be like: Many people choose to forgo plastic bags. Thus the industry would use new natural substances, e.g. cellulose.

In so doing something has changed ethically. Plastic bags will no longer pollute the Earth. Do you feel the power inherent in every human being?

Many people with a similar orientation for the welfare of mankind and the environment, will change whole industrial productions.

Ethically, you can reorient yourselves. You can lift nature, Earth, and animals into lighter, purer vibrations. The vibration of light influences the ethics among humans. Since lies will be detected by the high energy in the years to come, you can set new ethical standards. All systems are affected by the ethical clarification. This results in a lighter purified vibration on Earth. Thus the yardsticks of life will be raised, and the ethical orientation will also apply to the animal world (industrial live-stock farming), nature (deforestation for timber consumption), the use of chemicals (in crops, industrial plastics), the oceans (pollution), the earth (exploitation of resources, storage of waste) and much more. All areas of life will be affected by ethics and regarded as coherent systems. Please be aware of these necessary changes.

Thus, and only thus will you change your society for the better.

Is there anything better than living beings feeling comfortable, and that all species, including people, enter into a harmonious symbiosis?

Working together with the light vibrations, the spiritual world is striving towards this ethical transformation. Now!

Do not wait for someone else, start with yourselves.

Respect the water from your faucet, do not waste it. Respect nature as a living being, respect the biodiversity, do not carelessly throw your garbage away.

Sense the souls of your animals and sense the quality of life in the way they are kept.

When the concept of ethics is better understood by conscious people, it can also be implemented well. Then you raise your levels of clarification and purity. Analysing the term 'ethics' leads you to a clear spiritual attitude and its implementation in the outer world. All areas of life will benefit from the raise in ethics. On a small scale, these processes are already being practised on Earth. Mass awareness creates rapid changes, which is now starting. Look forward to these changes.

You think the lie per se does not mean much.

But you are wrong!

A lie is always either a manipulation or the fear of being discovered. I want to elucidate this topic, which is closely related to ethics.

A lie has the appearance of truth, but is not the truth at all.

What seems to be, but is not, turns out to be an illusion when looked at closely. It is a mirage. A lie presents an illusion of the truth. The spheres of light expose this illusion. Many people are already sensitive and are able to feel and expose a lie. The vibrational frequency enables them to feel what is true and what not. Lies intended to conceal have a very low frequency. Truthfulness has a high light vibration.

When communicating, many children can recognise these vibrational frequencies. In conversation, even adults who are highly energized recognise the lower energies of lies. In the years to come, more and more people will increase their energy field (refining and clarifying processes) and expose lies. This transparency in communication will change everything. The media, politics, just everybody will be exposed when concealing information.

Thus your global communication will be purified and cleansed. A great wave of cleansing will seize everyone. When a lie is detected, concealment is unnecessary.

So everyone is raised through truth. As a result of this higher frequency, authentic behaviour will prevail!

He who walks in truth, walks with God towards the light.

Love in your heart and good will to all men.

Love is the divine vibration of light, which has always existed on Earth. It has always been a high-level frequency. Those on Earth who worked on themselves and strived to live more consciously found their way into this energy.

High vibrational energy fields existed in all cultures. They were provided with divine light from the universe and could be activated by mankind using the vibration of light, and anyone who desired this could access them. At present, the irradiation is almost everywhere, and everyone is being pervaded by it, more or less.

When you feel love in your heart, you open your energy gates (chakras) and allow the vibration of love/light to flow into your body systems. Each cell is pervaded and gears itself more actively. Thanks to the vibration of love, it has always been possible for you on Earth to learn and to recognise – consciously. This has always been a voluntary possibility.

At present, each of you is being penetrated by light waves, and you no longer recognise nor understand yourselves. Open your heart, allow the light waves in, and the change will take place more easily. Your heart is the control centre for the love and the light within you. This love energy heals the body, and opens the doors of the hearts of others.

The power of love is strong, divine and all-encompassing. It is the help which the soul received for life on Earth to connect itself to the universal light energy. This energy of love for yourself accepts all parts of you and does not judge. Peace on all levels of the body.

The mind does the opposite, it criticises. In contemporary societies, the mind has gained a lot of power and is dominant. You place value on a clear, analytical mind, which can resolve all situations.

Love, too, sees the situation, but does not judge. It wraps it in peace and hope.

Hope, a part of love, needed many lives, in many cultures, to enable us to endure and to persist.

Those who love themselves and other people do not give up. They proceed with the certainty that everything is done truthfully. Those in love float on a pink cloud, as the saying goes. The problems are of no importance, everything can be solved. Confidence and faith proceed from the pink cloud. Love includes trust in life. You abandon yourself to love and allow yourself to be borne. Trust in God, the universe, and 'all that is'. Love is positive through and through, for the body and thus for each cell.

Self-love is often confused with selfishness.

To love yourself means accepting yourself and being at peace with yourself, being happy and satisfied. Those who can love themselves can love others, accept, respect, and appreciate them.

It is necessary to love yourself first; to accept and appreciate yourself. Those who are able to do this, will be able to face other people open-heartedly, with love. Your love relationships are perfect examples of love. In the family, love for partners and children is lived 'Thank God' (with God's help). You develop a love relationship to pets.

This vibration of the heart opens all doors. To encounter with love means being non-judgmental and living joyously. This energy heals all diseases and anguish, too. Love has a high vibration and was difficult for you to uphold permanently. Today and in the years to come, light waves will change this. You are being prepared to vibrate at such a high level of love energy permanently. All body systems are hereby cleansed and cleared and thus elevated.

It has now become possible to permanently sustain this energy of love. The body has already been prepared for this, or will be shortly.

Have trust!

Love is *the* energy of the new era.

Where love prevails, many things will heal by themselves and be exalted. The spiritual world will help boost the energy. Rejoice, many things will become easier. Go with love and free yourselves.

Raise your consciousness using the energy of love, share it with others. Thus they too will follow the path of love. This is the only way you will be able to change your society in the foreseeable future.

Master Kuthumi greets you from the radiant spheres, and lends support in all clearing processes. Help from God on all levels.

A question concerning hunting.

How is the hunting of animals to be defined ethically?

From my perspective of timelessness, I see that the matter of hunting will be cleared in the new era. For animals and for you people.

Hunting, the fact that people go hunting and fishing and return with a prey, has existed since the dawn of humanity.

Formerly, people used to kill animals because they believed them to be enemies, and felt threatened. Development progressed with time, and necessity (safety measure) turned into intention to make prey. All parts of the animal were utilized and processed for the requirements of life. Meat was important to the diet. People felt the strength which meat eating lent the body, and believed that the strength of the animal was transferred to them.

When an animal dies, as with a human being, the energy is released at the moment of death. Hoping to capture this energy, people ate the flesh of the animal believing that they would imbibe the entire strength of the slain animal.

This development thus turned people into meat eaters and predators.

Hunting became a group experience and strengthened the cohesion of the group of people.

Formerly, when hunting, people had to rely on each other; it was a social activity.

However, the groups killed only a few animals.

They were aware of the souls of the animals, respected them and, in awe, thanked them with rituals.

In your modern life, hunting and fishing have become sports with the power (money) to kill with a rifle or fishing rod; without struggle, without hardship, without a recognizable background. The meat is eaten, often not, while the trophy remains the hunter's triumph. Respect for the animal soul is lost. The belief that an animal is a second-class soul is an error.

The animal soul did not pass through the gate of oblivion when incarnating.

Animals are aware of their previous lives and that they will be at home, in the light, after physical death.

Animals live with the awareness of the coming and going, from and into Oneness.

Firing a shot, as a sport, in order to prey on animals is a primitive act.

With the current growing awareness you will change your attitude to hunting and understand the role animals have on Earth. The practice of hunting on a 'small' scale, i.e. taking care of 'hunting grounds' as you call it, is unnecessary. The animal populations regulate themselves, people need not intervene.

The mindset should change, for you and wildlife.

The needless killing of wild animals burdens your soul with guilt.

This hunters have to cleanse themselves of.

The knowledge and awareness of the importance of these processes, cleanses the actions and procedures, reducing guilt.

Animals are generally willing to sacrifice themselves to serve as meat when they recognise the humans' need. They open themselves to people and allow the meat to be taken; even wild animals do this. Mentally, telepathically animals should be asked. After the hunt, the ritual of thanks is very important for both souls; animals and humans can part in peace.

A high level of responsibility is required from future hunters, as well as the knowledge and understanding of the animal soul.

If you control the wild animal population by killing, nature responds with a higher birth rate (preservation of the species). Wild animals regulate their population themselves to the extent that food is available.

Animals bred for this purpose are aware of the intent, and accept it.

In my opinion, factory farming falls into the same category as hunting as a sport does.

May divine light and love enlighten human and animal souls collectively.
Master Kuthumi

Master Hilarion brings
messages of healing

I am Master Hilarion and serve on the green energy ray.
I greet you, you children on Earth, my messages are intended to help
you understand what healing is and how it is possible.

You seek physical and mental healing!

Healers have always existed in your cultures, medicine men and women
were needed to perform rituals and to contact the spiritual world.

Now you have doctors, hospitals, medical practitioners and many more.

Doctors are academic practitioners in the field of medicine and you
accept them as 'healers'. They help using drugs and various therapies.
The sick are congregated in hospitals so they can be better taken care
of. In your opinion, these institutions are necessary because all tools
and equipment are available there. The energy in hospitals is very low,
because there are many suffering people seeking help.

The suffering in these institutions is potentiated, and at auric level (the energy body surrounding each one) it encompasses the visitors and the workers there.

The energies comprise despair, emotional and physical distress, lack of understanding, a lot of pain - suffering at all levels.

This is what the vibration feels like in these congregations of the sick, in these hospitals.

Medical practitioners have a different training; compared to doctors they employ therapies with natural products. They utilize the healing powers of plants, minerals, oxygen, autologous blood, and many more.

There are also chiropractors who knowledgably try to align the skeletal system.

Osteopaths work with 'energy buttons' in the body in order to restore balance in its various systems.

In other cultures, there are medical treatments like acupuncture, oil applications, shamanic incantations, treatments with fire, and many more.

The new light vibrations reaching the Earth bring new methods of healing.

As physical and mental energy changes, i.e. rises to a higher level, medicine with a higher frequency becomes necessary. For healing only occurs when the cure or medicine has a higher vibrational power than the body to be healed.

Please note that healing necessitates a high vibration, an energy with a high potency!

Your homeopathy works with high potencies, Bach flowers are high potency drops.

Many chemically produced drugs will be less effective in the years to come; there is no fault with the medicine, but it is due to the elevated energies/vibrations of the body. For the present time of change, you need other methods to cure. Your medicine should quickly recognize and adapt to this.

In the plant world many high-vibrational healing options still lie dormant; please test these and use them.

In the next few years, there will be many discoveries in the field of botany. Messages from the spiritual world via channellings will assist you in the development of therapeutic medicine.

Hospitals must change into centres of healing. It takes a lot of heightened energy to heal the great number of patients. In the centres there should be rivulets, bird-song, healing music, energetic healing plants, crystals, and joy. The centres should be meeting places of highly potentiated vibration so that healing immediately becomes possible at all levels.

Health practitioners and natural healers should go in search of new insights in order to target the healing powers of the body more effectively. A few good ideas already exist in Eastern cultures.

Healing with energy, organizing it to meet the needs of each patient, is your challenge for the future.

Now already and more so in the future, it will be necessary to address all levels of the body in order that healing may occur.

The body itself is matter whose cells are in the process of elevation, of being enlightened.

With the energy irradiation from 2012 to 2020, this elevation is proceeding rapidly.

The energy system surrounding the body, called the aura, also increases its vibrational frequency.

Then there is the soul, (the spark of God), which already vibrates at a very high level.

The soul wishes to be recognised by the body, perceived consciously.

These are challenges which will not only change your life, but will decidedly change everything with regard to healing.

New methods of healing will quickly make their way to you thanks to the elevation of awareness.

Methods of healing of ancient cultures such as Lemuria and Atlantis will become available again.

Old diseases such as cancer, AIDS and bone diseases will be alleviated and occasionally completely healed. Cancer has evolved into a widespread disease. This is due to the disharmony between body and soul.

This will be recognised over the years and dealt with accordingly.

The numerous chemotherapies destroy your body enzymes, and it takes a long time and requires a lot of strength to restore the body.

In the future, cancer therapies will be therapies of consciousness and will require a fundamental change in the living conditions as well as in the patients' thought processes.

Cancer is curable if the patient so wishes.

On the other hand, many souls can use the disease of cancer to leave their bodies; this possibility will continue to exist.

Bone diseases due for surgery should first be scrutinized for attachments by foreign souls. The attachment of souls (deceased persons) in the aura of a body is a phenomenon of your present time.

Often the soul of a deceased relative or friend adheres to a person.

This mostly happens out of love, and fear that the person needs support in life - the adhering soul assumes. These souls have not ascended into the light, but remain earthbound looking for a host.

It happens for different reasons. Some souls become lodged in the large joints (in the aura). After some time, the host experiences pain in these joints. Classical medicine often has no clear explanation. Because of the pain, the joint is operated on in order to see what has caused the pain.

Here healers or initiated persons are required who recognise the attachment of souls and lovingly dismiss them into the light. The work demands a high level of consciousness and should be performed by trained persons. Once the adhering soul has been released, the pain and discomfort will disappear within a few days.

Surgery is unnecessary. It is a blessing for the soul to be recognised and released into the Light, and for the patients who can live their lives freely again, free from pain. Already this is a new method of healing which should be propagated to avoid unnecessary suffering.

Healing with energy is a topic of the new era.

Few people are already able to do so. It will spread quickly once the successes become well-known. Every person can make use of energy for themselves; the question 'how' can be explained:

The universal light and healing energy is available to everyone.

Transmission into the body is possible through the chakras.

Chakras are energy vortices of the body, which are present in everyone's aura.

Visual presentation of the aura and chakras.

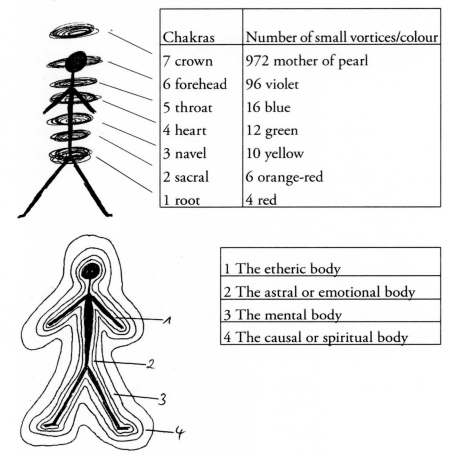

Chakras	Number of small vortices/colour
7 crown	972 mother of pearl
6 forehead	96 violet
5 throat	16 blue
4 heart	12 green
3 navel	10 yellow
2 sacral	6 orange-red
1 root	4 red

1 The etheric body
2 The astral or emotional body
3 The mental body
4 The causal or spiritual body

The chakras should be active and energetically balanced. To sense, feel or see this requires expert guidance. Presently, there are already healers who understand and implement this.

Through the crown chakra, bright light flows into the body, light which nourishes and heals the body. Through the root chakra, the energy from Mother Earth is absorbed; this energy too has a nourishing, healing and stabilizing effect on the body. Both energies, united in the body, can bring about healing on all levels of the body.

For the future of mankind, it is a basic method of healing, clearing, expansion and the elevation of consciousness. Working with chakras, the knowledge and understanding of the energy vortices are the cornerstones of the healing method of the future.

Healing with tones and natural sounds (birdsong, dolphin sounds, ocean sounds, and many more) are a new means of clearing of diseases. Tones or sounds penetrate into the deeper energy layers, arouse them, and result in reorientation. In this way, the body realigns itself and healing occurs. Mantra chanting (chanting of the monks) penetrates the cells and the subconscious mind promoting harmony and healing; it activates self-healing.

Self-healing is already in use today through various methods. This will change in the next few years, and a lot of knowledge will be added.

Healing with water is already known to you; the use of plant juices, vegetable oils and plant extracts is well-known too. These therapies will be intensified. They are means of promoting health.

Working on self-awareness – contacting the spiritual world and the spiritual guide of the individual in order to find out what is wrong with the patient – will be an effective way of understanding and recognizing the background of a disease in the future.

This method was used in ancient cultures to quickly recognize the emotional background of a disease. Even in the present day, knowledge of energy healing is available. It is applied sporadically and is very effective.

A disease often, almost always, occurs when the soul suffers, when it has strayed from its chosen path, does not know what to do, or suffers due to other circumstances which cause unhappiness. When this is recognised and understood in the application of healing methods, healing begins.

Client-centred therapies which take this knowledge into account bring about healing quickly. Contacting the soul on the spiritual level and investigating the origin of the problem is the easiest and fastest method of researching the cause. Contacting the spiritual plane is work done on the level of consciousness, which will be understood and taught in the new era.

Where illness exists, old thought and life patterns should always be checked, reflected, and changed for the benefit of the patient. In the years to come nervous disorders will multiply. This is normal due to the increased irradiation and may be associated with the physical cleansing processes. Drinking lots of water, eating fruit and vegetables, adequate rest and light exercise are helpful.

Tea brewed from common horsetail, and magnesium taken with water alleviate the disorders.

The strong light waves wish to penetrate the body, which results in pressure on all physical levels.

Using the treasures of Mother Earth in healing will be a crucial approach in medicine. Crystals and stones are energetic 'keys'. With these 'keys', you can reverse the polarity of pathogenic energies. You can energetically charge the water with stones so that it becomes healing water. All blockages in the body can be released by placing crystals on them. Different crystals have different effects. Using crystals, the chakras can be energised and activated. With the help of stones, dark spots and bands can be removed from the body. Crystals powerfully regenerate and harmonise the body, and balance it naturally.

Stones carry ancient information and readily pass it on. Just consider how long stones have grown, and how old they must be.

In the years to come, Mother Earth will open her large crystal fields. Thus there will be sufficient stones/crystals for all humanity. Mother Earth offers her medicine to her children in the form of crystals.

Crystals cut differently have different effects. Some have a purifying, invigorating effect, while others increase the vibration of the aura, or activate the mental capacity and support the body in many ways. Try it out, just let yourself go, it is that simple.

Stones have souls, and look forward to communicating with your consciousness and working with you. Large stones are like power plants, for yourself and the environment. The variety of crystals/ stones creates unprecedented opportunities; thus consciousness will make everything possible. The size of the stone will always be important energetically. Large stones are intended for large halls and spaces, and energize the aura of everyone present in the halls/spaces. The stones raise the vibrational field of the people present, effecting healing and harmony. Unnoticed by them, their energy is raised to correspond with that of planet Earth.

Crystals placed in water activate, cleanse, and transform molecules. Take particular notice of these statements. With knowledge and awareness you can cleanse all the water from all pollutants. Infested oceans, nuclear water would be a manageable task. We from the spiritual world will guide you.

Crystals can also be specially programmed. They can be charged to undertake a specific action in order to obtain a desired effect. Make enquiries, there are people around today who heal and energise using crystals. Stones work together with the chakra system: energy (stone) and energy (vortex). Through the aura, stones have an effect on the physical level due to the molecular structure of their solid matter. Communication with crystals is possible, if you allow it.

Healing with the power of thought and believing in healing is a therapy with a high measure of self-involvement. You can support your thoughts with affirmations such as 'I am healthy', 'I heal myself', 'I'm fine', and many more.

Repeat these affirmations several times per day; thus the subconscious mind is guided into believing what is said, and accepts it as being true.

Then the body programs itself to heal by mobilising its healing powers. Healing in this way works when faith and confidence in its success are present. If you have faith in yourself and believe in your own strength during this therapy, healing takes place on all levels.

This process requires inner clarity and the courage to take responsibility for yourself.

However, you willingly forego the responsibility for your illness giving it to your doctor or therapist expecting help and healing by means of internal and external applications. This is a fundamental error! Healing can only take place inside of you, through recognition and clarification of the pathogenic circumstances in which you live. Grievances may lie dormant in your system for many years. They do not cause pain, but remain unobtrusive. Then, all of a sudden, they emerge through pain, fears, blockages, depression, thoughts and accidents, and you ask, 'what's wrong now?' Now the time has come to clarify everything. The past, the burdens, the stress, deprivation and suffering wish to be reviewed, addressed, and released. The light waves of the new era bring to light what has been repressed, so that it can be reviewed, addressed, and released.

Now too the time has come for souls on Earth who have been trapped on Earth's etherial level for many years, to make their presence felt. Why do they want to be noticed just now? The energies of Earth are gradually increasing, and these souls (these physical blockages or unsolved family matters) have no other alternative but to seek clarification, for fear of being seen through, and recognised. What has not been clarified perceives the light and wishes to be released, finally, so it makes itself felt. Cleaning up in all areas of life works in this way too.

The bright divine light permeates all levels so that they can be raised.

Whoever wishes to ascend and reach the next level, first has to conclude the level on which they find themselves, to overcome all challenges and manage all fields of learning. As you know, this is how computer games are organized, and this is how the ascension into the next dimension will come to pass.

Now it is time for you to address the fields of learning, your ancestry, what has been repressed, etc. Looking the other way or ignoring it has now become impossible.

Those of you who refuse to take the path of clarification, for whatever reason, are free to do so (your free will matters!). They will be reborn in order to re-address the fields of learning; then, maybe, with more strength and courage, possibly in other life situations making it easier. Please read this non-judgementally, because everyone has the right to make their own decisions, always!

In a few years, eating habits will change. The raise of consciousness will induce this. Your body, the cells will be more filled with light, will be brighter, requiring a light diet.

Ideologically, this transformation will hardly be possible. The body will send signals regarding nutrition, and mankind will respond accordingly.

As the era advances, the body will require inedia (feeding on photons of sunlight, breathing and metabolizing it), but there will be a long period of transition, extending over many decades.

Inedia, is not an issue yet.

On a voluntary basis, of course, you can try this out, and if you wish, you can change. But please, quite voluntarily, and only if you feel strong and your body feels comfortable.

The general change is as follows :

The body will need a little more sugar to calm the nerves and to maintain balance. Food which is hard to digest, fat, all fast food, too many carbohydrates, and meat will increasingly cause problems in the digestive tract, and also nausea.

Only by experiencing these physical symptoms will we become aware of this change.

A light diet, all kinds of fruit, is quickly digested and supplies the body with the required fructose. Vegetables in the terrestrial diversity are varied, filling, and strengthen the body with enzymes, minerals and vitamins. Meat can be avoided, fish can be consumed; in moderation it is digestible.

The intake of food will be reduced; this is related to the irradiation of energy on Earth. The light waves reach Earth in intervals; in the years 2012 to 2021, the intensity of the waves will increase very slowly and will progressively influence the human system. The intake of food will decline almost unnoticeably. You will eat many small meals, which will be more digestible.

In the new era, the world population will be able to feed itself!

Fruits, seeds, nuts, and plants will be available in abundance and will be very nutritious and tasty. You will convert your water into healing water.

Alcohol, drugs, and cigarettes will be recognised as narcotics for the masses and will become less important due to people's awareness.

The changes have already started, whether you choose to accept or decline.

Tune in to the new era. You will gain a better understanding and be able to heal yourself.

You recognise many changes and are pleased with the progress which benefits all people, animals, and Mother Earth.

With the energy of love, I, Master Hilarion, support and guide you in your process of transformation.

Lady Nada connects with the feeling of love

Live the love which is in your heart, and you flow with life.
Lady Nada, the master of the ruby red ray of energy speaks to you.

Empathy is the grace of the heart which allows you to feel.

Just sense, 'What is the other person feeling?' Empathy, sensing, unmasks many delusions and traumas. Sensing, empathizing, is applied to others. It is the gift to experience what others are feeling. You have always been trained - by yourselves and the spiritual world - to develop this empathy. It is a way of communicating from the heart which reaches the heart of others. People who empathize with others identify with their life circumstances. Often, empathy is a snapshot. Generally, a momentary impression prevails. A situation arises, is perceived by one's empathy, and triggers the energy flow from the heart.

'I sympathize with you' is a strong statement from the heart. It is beneficial for your community to be compassionate. This feeling unites you, and in that moment you accept that you are all 'one'. The closeness of the heart creates this sense of unity, to the benefit of all involved.

Showing compassion, pitying another, is also a feeling which emanates from the heart. In your heart you suffer with others. Suffering has a low vibration, which damages the heart. Feeling pity penetrates the heart deeply. You take the suffering of another upon yourself. Many people who suffer with the sufferer remove some of their burden. Thus the sufferers can feel free again; unconsciously they have handed over part of their suffering allowing the relief. In their heart the fellow sufferers now carry part of the suffering of another. This suffering is not their own; they cannot resolve it. These negations indicate that this compassion, this 'act of suffering', is problematic. It causes problems in the systems of your body for how will you rid yourself of the suffering of another? You can work through your own. Your system is not meant to clear foreign suffering. Please do not adopt foreign suffering!

Suffering belongs to the person who is supposed to work through it, to grow, and to mature.

Empathizing is a good way of showing sympathy. Compassion hinders your body and your mind.

May God bless you wherever you go.

This I wish with all my heart!

Blessing is a sign of great respect and appreciation, and unites with love and good fortune in all areas of life.

Blessing, bestowing blessing or good wishes is a sacred act.

Divinity is inherent in 'giving a blessing'.

Regardless of what is now or will be in the future, mankind, actions and situations, the home and job, and everything else were blessed. Everything was considered and was granted good wishes for the future.

What then results, depends on what the individual makes of it. You have a high degree of freedom. Good wishes are not subject to any requirements.

Blessing means freedom in thought and deed. Bestowing a blessing is generally a religious act and is associated with the blessing of God. However, anyone can bestow a blessing. All of you can bless something or someone else, freely and without any ceremony. After all, a blessing is an energetic wave of light which brightens and raises everything wished for. It is recommended that you bless your food and the acquired nourishment daily, thus making it particularly digestible and wholesome. This is blessing unto yourselves.

A blessing is an extremely clear energy of love which can work wonders.

Blessing children and adults is the highest frequency of light and love, and is strong and protective.

Bestow blessings in your life more frequently – since you now know the meaning thereof. Use this kind of blessing to manifest light frequencies; use it for yourself and for others.

Grace is a word whose meaning is interpreted in different ways. I shall hereby make the universal meaning clear. Being gracious, merciful, means being lovingly gentle, non-judgmental. Being free from assessment, accepting at face-value, without enquiring whether something is true or not. Accepting it as such, graciously. Grace means: a blessing combined with gratitude. To accept gratefully what has been blessed. To thank the blessing. *To practise grace*, to regard something gently and lovingly, to give thanks for it, thus setting it free. Grace is blessed gratitude and acceptance of what is.

If in your cultures thoughts of grace are thought more often, many conflicts and disputes dissipate of their own accord.

Tuning in to the energy of grace has gone out of fashion in your Western cultures. Please return to this so-called old-fashioned way of thinking. It will make many things easier, more peaceful.

Be merciful towards yourselves and others, accepting non-judgmentally and thanking that things are the way they are.

The power of grace is a loving, fatherly energy, the energy of 'God the Father'.

Life in large and small communities has always existed in your countries and cultures.

I want to tell you what life on Earth can be like with the new light energy - in communities and among each other.

Today you live in families. Children are born, brought up, and then they create their own lives. They leave the parental home. Older people go to residential communities or retirement homes, living separately until life ends. Many people live alone seeking social contacts. In rural or poorer areas, life in the extended family still exists, mostly based on kinship relationships, which bind for life.

People living alone have withdrawn from the family unit, living their lives according to their individual needs. In extended families, living together is only possible when compromises are made, and everybody's role is specified. People who have chosen to be single wish to try this out.

Along with the new energy vibrations, new life-mode arrangements will appear in the minds of the people.

Communal life comes to the fore, as it promises many benefits for each individual.

Awareness is trained and produces good ideas. Rethink your life-style, a change is always possible.

The future will bring forth communities who think and act liberally.

Many people who share similar interests will get together to work on the same projects, having equal rights. This will give rise to a centre where people with different ideas, will create an object, topic, or product holistically, complementing each other. From these working groups, living communities will develop where acceptance and liberality will be prevalent. It is self-evident that families will come into being there, and several generations will live and work together. These communities will be joined by other communities with complementary or other projects. This creates a vast working and residential area. People often stay there for a lifetime, with the freedom to meet new challenges at any time.

The occupation is a vocation, an interest, a hobby, a passion, and will be lived as such.

Occupations as you know them today will undergo a change. At present you mostly learn and study for a profession/occupation. In the future you will sense your skills and tendencies in childhood already. As a child you will already be encouraged and challenged so that your interest becomes a calling, which will then be realised as a *vocation*. This type of shaping one's occupation will sustain the joy and interest in the activity. Changing one's occupation will be possible at all times, and will be seen as trying out something and as gaining knowledge. The entire field of occupation will offer more freedom, and will consequently be less stressful. The individual will not need to orient themselves towards the wages; the income of the community will be shared fairly so that everyone has their livelihood.

The system focuses on voluntary unity, where room for individuality is maintained. Many years will pass before these modes of living and working come to pass.

I wish to instruct you about the upbringing of children now and in the new era.

In various cultures on different continents, you bring up your children according to different models.

In the Western world, in America and Europe, children live according to models which have to be, and therefore are, explained scientifically.

In child care centres and schools, the way children are dealt with depends on the personal attitude of the educators, the teachers and the supervisors. Of course, you are committed to the models followed, but the individual implementation lies with the person performing them.

No explanation is needed when it comes to modes of schooling and education. They are all alike.

Dealing with children and adolescents on the basis of love is the crucial pivotal point for a positive change.

Children and adolescents born from 1990 and thereafter differ in behaviour and conduct from children in former times.

You talk of Indigo, Aquarius and Star children, children of the new age, who impact differently on their environment. They have difficulty orienting themselves on Earth, and are sensitive beings. They are often maladjusted, even rebellious or too introverted.

Externally, they differ greatly, but this they all share: they are all mentally alert, intelligent and mostly clairsentient, clairvoyant or clairaudient. These children are born with these gifts. In kindergartens and schools, people are reluctant to notice these skills because they feel insecure in dealing with these children. Therefore they are treated according to the norm. The behaviour of the adults makes them feel insecure, makes them withdraw, or makes them aggressive. The *new children* feel misunderstood, marginalized, and often rejected. Today already, teachers and caregivers should have knowledge of this new generation of children, they should accept them and learn to guide them. If these new-age children are treated and instructed properly and heartily accepted, great things can be expected from them. They are ready (incarnated on Earth for this purpose) to create freedom in society and the economy. You need these new children!

If they are misunderstood and maltreated, they will wither and fail to live up to their duties. That would be a great loss!

The souls of these children have incarnated from other galaxies, from Lemuria, Atlantis and from the spiritual world and have very definite goals to assist with the ascension of the Earth. You need them! Please treat them wisely and justly so that they can live their full potential.

In secondary schools, these children stand out due to their keen minds and quick wit. If they are well accepted by their parents and guided lovingly, they will follow their path and learn to live their life's purpose. The home is the cornerstone to becoming a holistic being (the integration of body, mind, and life purpose) for these souls. Often the parents are aware of their children's special qualities, and accept them lovingly.

The spiritual world brings these parents into contact with spiritual people who explain what these children are like, and who help them to understand them. You think these are coincidences, but coincidences do not exist.

Mostly parents start their spiritual journey triggered by the influence of their children.

Loving acceptance of these new children is particularly important. For love enables them to feel at home quickly and to understand the circumstances on Earth. They come from spiritual spheres and often it is their first incarnation on Earth, yet they are old souls, or even souls of masters and priests. For dealing with the souls of such children, this knowledge is very helpful.

Many of the new children bring joy and wisdom to Earth, bringing a blast of fresh air into families, kindergartens, and schools. This is intended; thus people around them learn to question themselves and to reflect. Learning processes are set into motion by the conduct of these children. In the eyes of these children, you often look deeply into your own souls, and your heart is moved. This emotion is intended; it is the only way for you to sense your heart and to open it to the energy of love - for yourselves and life in general.

When children are born, you give them a name. Each name has an energetic vibration and enhances or limits the child, depending on the intensity of the vibration. Find out about numerology and consciously choose the name according to the degree of vibration which you wish your child to have.

In numerology each letter has a specific numerical value; the sum total results in a number with a specific meaning allocated to the name. Very often the mother or father senses a name during pregnancy, and this is generally the appropriate name for the baby. Through their names, children identify with themselves and accept themselves as terrestrial, individual personalities. Your calendars have saints days. These names too can be useful approaches for naming a child.

A feeling is a message which your body sends in order to draw your attention.

This feeling comes from the heart centre and can vary in intensity. Then feelings differ: joy, sadness, happiness, fear, and many more. You experience feelings daily. A feeling is initiated by the soul and then speaks from your heart. It evokes memories, startles, makes you pause; briefly said, it teaches you. Through a feeling your behaviour changes, in one or the other direction. Feeling teaches the mind to act. The other way round, information is processed haltingly. The mind is startled by the feeling, and begins to ponder, to explore, and to question - what or why? A feeling, the message from the soul, makes the contact between body and soul possible.

If you internalize this, you can communicate with your soul and explore what makes it happy. Then, please, be happy!

Being happy, feeling happy is a good feeling which makes the body vibrate harmoniously. Harmony heals the body.

Laughing, a smile is also an expression of the soul.

When meeting someone, looking into their face, into their eyes, smile. It is a greeting from your soul to the other soul. Thus it pleases you and the other person too because you have recognised each other in the depths of the universe.

Perhaps this encounter from soul to soul, even if it lasts only seconds, is a lingering recognition.

A smile, a greeting sent to an acquaintance or a stranger, pleases your heart and increases the vibration of your body. Try it out, experience will teach you.

Sense the energy released by a smile. It is that easy.

Small gestures (a smile) can change entire societies.

In other (few) cultures this is already heeded, and when it comes from the heart, it is perfect.

Is not Japan called the Land of Smiles?

Smiling, I take my leave and wish to touch your soul in the depths of the universe. The Master, Lady Nada

10

The galactic master Ashtar Sheran sends photonic light rays for peace on Earth

I am the light vibration, Ashtar Sheran. I command the Grand Cosmic Squadron of universal peace.
My intent regarding mankind is to spread the message of light and peace.

The light body (aura) around your physical body will brighten in the years to come, and the frequencies in your aura field will increase. These great changes which the universe provides are inevitable and have already been initiated. Your internal as well as external physical structures are changing rapidly. Your thinking processes are only gradually adapting to the changes. The thoughts vibrate slower than the light (the colours) of your aura. You will change without being aware of what is happening to you. These are processes taking place universally. Every person is subject to this; the free will has no influence. On Earth there are and have always been people whose light bodies vibrate at a higher frequency. They usually work behind the scenes (with a few exceptions: Diana, Mother Teresa, Mahatma Ghandi, Nelson Mandela, and others) and avoid the media.

The light bodies of your physical body are developed by the chakras in the aura; they are opened and activated. This is how your light body unfolds on Earth. In the Third Dimension, from which the Earth *now* ascends, these energetic light bodies were not needed. Now, ascending into the 5th Dimension, the light bodies have become necessary to stabilize you energetically and enable you to live healthy lives on Earth in the future. The active light body makes you telepathic, clairsentient, clairaudient and clairvoyant. Communication is possible through thought. The veils of your true 'I Am' are removed. You will then know where you are going when you leave the Earth, and will know whence you came.

You are multidimensional!

A spark of Divinity!

The entire universe is your home!

You have bound yourselves to Earth by self-imposed and desired fields of learning. Each of you wished and wishes to experience life on Earth.

But Earth is just one place of learning in the universe.

The light body development of your human body:

Additional energy vortices (chakras) will be activated in your aura.

Due to the increasing light photons radiating from the sun to the Earth, two vortices will be activated over the head, and two under the feet. This will take place very gently according to the development of the individual.

The activated chakras will enable you to become more subtle and more sensitive.

The chakra at your feet will reveal the origin of your soul. Of your own accord (almost suddenly) you will know who you are. You experience yourselves as soul, body and mind, and sense the individual energy vortices (chakras).

The chakra approximately 25cm under your feet connects you with Mother Earth and anchors you terrestrially. All thoughts materialise visibly, and thinking becomes matter when this energy vortex is activated. What you think is realised!

So think consciously and responsibly.

The openings of the chakras under the feet enable the soul to effect something, utilising the energy of the Earth. Thoughts and ideas materialise.

The chakra a hand's breadth over the head, works together with the chakra under the feet and supports the knowledge concerning the origin of the soul. The understanding that you have already lived many lives on Earth and that your soul is immortal, is released by the active ion of this vortex over your head. A meditative look at previous lives thus becomes possible, for a better understanding and for your confirmation.

The chakra approximately 25cm over your head is called the gate of the soul. It becomes active when you are on the path to self-fulfilment and the question of God is raised. This vortex of energy establishes contact with the spiritual world, the Ascended Masters, archangels, unicorns, and with the divine power of the universe. Via this vortex you are connected to the Divine Light and are supplied with divine love from Oneness, Father-Mother God. You recognise your divinity!

In the years to come, all four chakras outside of your body (under your feet and over your head) will be activated gradually and individually in everyone by the energetic radiation of the sun. Through this activation you will be more aware and sensitive, your inner wisdom will reveal itself. The spiritual and the material worlds will become more permeable and you will be able to look into both worlds. The veils will be lifted and you will recognise and understand my messages.

Graphic representation of the physical and non- physical chakras :

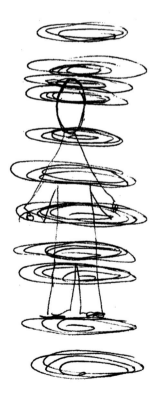

At present your galaxy is being observed by many spaceships of my fleet.

When we fly over the terrestrial energy gates, we become visible within them for a short while. Many people have already seen these brightly lit, mirrored surfaces of my spaceships and find diverse explanations of *what* they saw. In your films UFOs from other galaxies may appear. You may visualise this, but you ban it from reality, i.e. from real life.

We, the intergalactic spaceship fleet, are real and will soon be visible to many people. This text prepares you for it.

We have come to protect and help you.

Our mission is to implement the ascension of the Earth into the 5th Dimension, peacefully and according to the Divine Universal Plan. Interferences from outside, from other universes, are to be avoided. This important evolutionary step, the raising of your galaxy onto a higher vibrational energy level, is of great importance for the entire universe, and must transpire quietly and peacefully.

Monitoring this is our mission!

We take care of the external peace of your galaxy. Taking care of internal peace, peace on Earth, is the duty and challenge of the people on Earth. There have been great wars; they seem to have been overcome. There are still many smaller wars and conflicts. Please, get these problems under control as quickly as possible, settle the disputes. Spiritual masters and angels are present as mediators to cleanse the energy on Earth and to create peace. Male ego behaviour, supported by strong power structures is staged and tested martially in the so-called 'Middle East'.

Such power games with weapons and poison gas should be refrained from; this is unrewarding for the destination of the Earth. The wars on Earth are macho games and have always been instigated deliberately; stop these old games, they will not produce any new insights. In Asia the game 'who is stronger' is presently being played. These struggles and presentations are habits from the history of Earth, let go of them. Recognise that wars are instigated.

The wise women and men who bear political responsibility should recognise these games and have the courage to intervene, bringing about reconciliation. Who benefits from territorial games? You are ascending into the new world, into the dimension of Light.

It does not matter who owns what land; all of you live on the Earth and will restructure it after the processes of transformation. Your world will change within the next 20-30 years. Old land will be flooded, while new land emerges from the sea. Climatic turbulences and the cleansing process now pending on the Earth will jointly initiate the transformation. I hereby make this knowledge available for humanity.

What is the point of your macho games? Make peace, unite worldwide, and meet the challenges confronting you.

Weather phenomena and tectonic plate movements are the learning processes you have to expect in the near future.

Energy systems should be reconsidered and converted creatively (a few spiritual people get relevant information from the spiritual world; have the courage to try out their feasibility).

The water in and on the Earth needs to be cleansed! Large crystals can achieve this.

The storms devastating your planet increasingly should be appeased. Train people who can deal with the elements, who can cope with them. These are the new challenges you face on Earth. Old war games will become superfluous; you will have to master many challenges in the years to come. My squadron of cosmic light will help you; accept this help!

We protect the space, the aura surrounding your Earth, and can, if desired, intervene on Earth.

In order that we can help, you should accept and trust that I and the galactic fleets exist. We were sent to keep interferences away from the great ascent of the Earth.

My fleets maintain the energy of your universe at the level which you need to change the current circumstances. We are happy to help, if so desired, to make and preserve peace on Earth (at the energy level). Raise your consciousness so that you can see and hear us; this makes our help easier.

Your sun is the central energy of your galaxy.

You ought to understand it as a power plant. The sun is part of the solar system of the universe, of the Great Central Sun. Your sun is a spin-off, a spark of the Great Mother Sun, the all-embracing Divine Central Sun. Thus your sun is responsible for shaping your galaxy.

Its great consciousness makes life on Earth possible.

Its great consciousness creates knowledge, intelligence and consciousness on Earth.

Its great consciousness allows your power games.

Its great consciousness created your Earth as *Gaia* and provided Earth with consciousness.

Now this high universal consciousness of the sun is increasing and is drawing your galaxy along into the ascent. The sun, too, cleanses itself by means of processes in order to make the ascent for itself and the entire galaxy possible. These cleansing processes are implosions and explosions on and within the sun. The effects of this solar cleansing will soon be felt on Earth within the next few years. Each planet of your galaxy will be affected and prepared for ascension onto the next level by means of its own cleansing processes. The distance between the Sun and the Earth slows down the current process. The effects of these implosions and explosions reach you on Earth years later.

They are already on their way.

We notice these vibrations and are aware of the energy which will hit the Earth. Your scientists call them solar winds and they are already familiar with this topic. The media have partial knowledge of these solar winds, but withhold the information in order to placate the public.

When the winds/solar winds or even geomagnetic storms reach Earth, you will recognise them by the orange/red discolouration of the sky. Prepare yourselves communally and fortify what you can. The solar winds carry higher temperatures. The heat will be unusual for planet

Earth, but will soothe all human systems and cause tiredness. Many people will sleep through these winds, which is good!

The crucial impact will have to be carried by the water of your planet.

The winds address the oceans' consciousness causing them to expand.

The oceans, lakes and rivers occupy more space and a larger surface. All coastal regions will be timeously informed (spiritual messages will be scientifically confirmed) and will take appropriate action. These announcements, hereby made known, are true and should be considered. When the winds ebb, the water will withdraw only minimally; it will maintain its territory. Land will have been flooded in all parts of the world and this will remain so. The oceans, lakes and rivers will have been purified by the winds and will thus be ready for ascent. This measure is necessary and has been initiated.

After the great phase of transformation, the weather will normalise gradually.

Constant temperatures will dominate.

The seasons as you know them in parts of the world, will disappear almost completely.

It will be said that the weather on Earth is almost constant and calm. The time of the great winds and erratic weather will be over. Then your life will be more consistent, and steady.

After the ascent into the new dimension, the sun will have gained in clarity and will exude this to Earth. You will sense the sun as being brighter, bringing more clarity and order within you. The light of the sun lights up your cells and increases your awareness. The changes in solar radiation will pacify your nervous system and you will vibrate harmoniously.

During this phase of transition on your planet, everyone will be in their designated place. We from the spiritual spheres will protect and guide you so that everyone can perform the task they have assumed for this life in order to participate in the ascension. You will all be in the right place at the right time, exactly where you are needed. This has been predetermined.

Your Earth cleanses itself from within; you have noticed this in recent years. Many earthquakes demonstrate this to you on the surface of the Earth. They may increase in intensity. At the interfaces of the tectonic plates, movements and turbulences will persist. Adapt the development of residential areas accordingly, and settle in calm locations on your planet. Volcanoes will be more active; they will conduct the internal pressure of the Earth to the outside easing the tension of the terrestrial system. Accept the cleansing processes of the Earth; after many thousands of years, this is overdue and has been pre-determined in order to achieve the ascension into the Fifth Dimension.

Your Earth has cleansed itself many times in order to be born again to then exist for thousands of years.

For eons, great energy gates have been installed on Earth.

These gates were used by the inhabitants of other galaxies and universes to visit the Earth. The different cultures on the planet show the effects of inter- and extra-galactic visits. You humans have been shaped by these multi- galactic influences. The light gates have been closed now during the ascent in order to avoid interference from outside. My light fleet has been assembled for this reason, to guard the gates and to keep attackers and curious visitors from other universes at bay. This ascension process requires a great amount of energy, and is to be mastered by Earth and all beings living on Earth. Our fleets, especially appointed by the Intergalactic Council, are responsible for a smooth discharge. My fleet and I have gladly accepted this assignment. We can assist you people whenever you wish. This has been predetermined. I herewith openly offer my assistance, and would enjoy being summoned. People who wish to communicate with me are welcome to do so. Please call my name, wait for the light, then ask your questions, and listen to the answers. My fleet and I look forward to this.

Many children with new/old souls communicate with our fleets and can also see them. They are aware of the role we play in the process of peace on Earth. We are responsible for peace, and for universal peace only.

The ships of my fleet could become visible if you wish to see them. You call this technique materialising. I, Ashtar Sheran, am ready and I am pleased to be able to introduce myself to you. This contact can be useful for you people because our ships are (for your imagination) over-dimensionally large and could accommodate thousands of people. The following should be considered: Our fleet is a fleet of light, so there are high energies within its system. People with an increased awareness physically tolerate these light frequencies, while people with lower frequencies might have problems with the light and might have to cope with pain and other symptoms.

I look forward to the contact with you.

Within your Earth, at great depths, unimaginable amounts of crystal fields are stored.

This information is not an invitation for exploitation and enrichment. Do not even think of power play and money games involving these crystals.

The large crystals have a clear, light-filled consciousness and would disintegrate into carbon – from which they are made. The consciousness of these crystals is so high that, using them, you can instantly heal. In the hands of responsible people they serve the entire world. After the ascension process, the Earth will release these crystal fields immediately. Using these crystals you will be able to generate electricity, put machinery in motion, heal the Earth, etc.

People with the relevant disposition should now already train and teach others to become aware of and understand the consciousness of these large crystals.

Your planet has a chakra system, and so do you.

These chakras are activated in quick succession in the years to come. The vibration of the sun radiating photons, and the consciousness of the people with their Heart Energy make this possible. In the year 2012, the first chakra was opened in England, and more are to follow. When all of Earth's chakras have been opened, the time is come for the ascent of the Earth.

There is no exact date for it is an evolutionary process. To enable Gaia to clear her chakras better and faster, you people can make contact with the Earth and perform healing rituals. This will please the Earth, and it will show its gratitude by being harmonious.

You are all connected to the Earth and can only ascend as a unit.

Look and see, we are all working towards the fulfilment of the Divine Plan.
Together we can make it.
I will lead you in divine love.
Ashtar Sheran

11

Maitreya, the energy of Christ on Earth, enlightens us on life and death

I Am Maitreya, the Cosmic Christ energy on your Earth.
My messages help you understand.
I wish to explain the topic of life and death to you.

The counterpart of dying is being born.

Through birth the soul enters into the world of matter.

Where does the soul live?

The soul lives, dwells, learns and trains itself 'at home'. The 'home' is groups of souls in the spheres of light. There, just being is important, simply being in profound peace. In other words: lightness and peace, harmony and joy - existence in nourishing divine light. The groups of souls are often composed of the same or similar fields of learning and developmental processes. Within the soul families/soul groups, there is only transparency. Figuratively speaking, everything is there, the life experiences of all the souls in the group are palpable and visible to every soul. The learning fields of soul groups are to be mastered communally and non-judgmentally, in a supportive and stimulating way. In soul families every soul can recuperate after a life on Earth; similarly the issues which are important for a new life on Earth are clarified. Strength, courage, joy and love are replenished, absorbed, in order to re-incarnate (be reborn, to incarnate). The whole soul group supports the new incarnations. They often offer a 'jump-start' and incarnate too. There are countless possibilities in the soul groups.

Soul families live in the vibrational energy of divine love and universal peace. The life of the soul 'at home' is difficult to explain because words are too superficial. The existence of the soul in the spheres of light is merely a vibration of light; you are correct in calling it 'paradise'.

If the soul chooses to incarnate on Earth (to assume a body), parents and family structures are sought in which the learning processes the soul has planned for its new life, can be well implemented. The soul chooses the parents, and incarnates.

Bleeding in early pregnancy or miscarriages in later stages of pregnancy indicate the departure of the soul. The soul withdraws its decision to incarnate. Or the soul has only chosen the early stage of pregnancy as the period of incarnation.

There is an infinite number of ways in which the soul can gain experience.

Please accept the decisions of the souls.

If the pregnancy goes well, and the child dies during birth or thereafter, that was all the soul intended to experience in this life; it was planned.

The soul lives according to its soul plan.

Whenever a child, a young or old person dies, it is because that soul chooses to leave the Earth.

To understand and to accept this in your heart is the learning process of each one.

When someone dies suddenly due to a misfortune or an accident, preparation for the transition into the spheres of light is unnecessary. The soul decided in favour of the sudden departure from the body. The soul plan is always fulfilled!

Many souls have a long period of preparation before leaving the body.

Long or short phases of illness make the process of detachment of the soul from the body predictable. During this time the soul detaches, often looking 'home' recognising the way to follow, and usually also the soul plan which has to be realised. To behold the light from 'paradise' makes the process of separation of soul and body easier, less fearful. It often occurs that the souls of departed friends and relatives appear to meet the soul of the person dying. These souls show themselves, and communicate with the soul who is still on Earth. They prepare the process of ascent.

Souls often need a long period of preparation in order to let go when the last breath has come. The soul then exits the body!

The body remains as an earthly 'house' and is returned to the Earth. The circle of life closes.

If a person has severe pain before dying, suffers from a serious illness, or suffers spiritual pain, acquired guilt/karma is eliminated through the pain, is dissolved and transformed. The spark of light, the soul, can then easily leave the body because the body is worn out.

The guilt was cleared.

Often family members need a longer time to take leave, so the soul remains in the diseased body waiting until its loved ones are willing and able to let go. The soul decides on this time management within the process of dying. There is rarely *a* date on which the soul can leave the body. There are usually several time windows through which the light spark can leave the Earth. Many souls remain trapped in the body because of heavy feelings of guilt. They wish to sort out what needs to be clarified. Such a process of dying may last long and be painful for the patient and for the relatives.

Dying, letting go of the physical shell is easiest when peaceful. A breath separates the life from the body. Via this breath you let go of everything earthly and advance to the bright spheres going 'home'.

The aging process of humans is a visible sign that it is time to think about life and death, and to deal with these issues. In ancient cultures people were aware of this period of life, and old people were called 'the wise'. They philosophized about life and its circumstances, and about other phenomena. Naming old age a period of wisdom should be reconsidered. Wise people are needed, they can guide and lead the younger ones and pass on their knowledge. In the new era all generations are needed to reshape the Earth.

The soul's process of ascent is well-known. It transpires through the energetic column of light, a kind of elevator, which leads to the Divine Light.

Weeks, days, or hours, often only seconds before death, the great angel of peace, also called the angel of transition, stands by the dying and guides them gently through the ritual of release. In this sacred process this angel maintains all energies lovingly and radiates the peace of God.

Lots of little angels, the Elohim, help the soul to leave the body, and guide the soul into the column of light so that it can find its way 'home'.

Imagine the soul as a small, very bright, glittering ball. Souls who are ill, are lovingly cared for and clarified in places of healing in the bright spheres before they can go 'home'. This is the description of an ideal separation process of a soul from its earthly life.

At present, many souls refuse the ascent into the light using the divine column of light. They prefer to remain earthbound. They believe they can solve their conflicts in a disembodied state. These are areas which the soul has chosen to experience. This is to be respected. Managing these earthbound tasks is difficult for the spark of light, the soul. Nevertheless, many souls choose to do so. Maybe they see it as a cleansing of karma and had planned it this way as part of the human experience (the free will on earth matters).

When the Earth rises into the Fifth Dimension, all earth-bound souls will be guided 'home', into the light.

Incarnation, rebirth, being born again, continues when the soul has chosen a new life in order to learn once more.

Thus, the spark of light starts afresh in a new body. The gender can be chosen as well as the skin colour and the continent on which the soul is to be born, and the culture as well. These are decisions the soul is free to make. The life path and the life purpose of a soul are important approaches for shaping life.

A child becomes an adolescent, who in turn becomes an adult. And soon you will have exceeded the zenith of life, and the question concerning the meaning of life will come up, and you will ask, 'Was that all?'

Many of your lives take this course and similar questions are asked.

We from the spiritual world tell you that life leads you to your life purpose, for this is what the soul has chosen.

How do you know what your life purpose is?

In most cases, there are many clues. From childhood on, you are shown where you should follow which path. The environment, influences of parents and friends, and idols which are regarded as role models, direct you.

When turning left at a crossroads in life, although you would reach your destination turning right, the life purpose will be more difficult to reach, or you may even miss it entirely (to illustrate a point). This is what many of your lives look like: you miss the purpose of life, i.e. the target the soul has set for that incarnation.

Then the soul assumes this goal for the next life again. It is difficult to recognise one's own life purpose and realise it. It seems that many interferences occur randomly in your life. The coincidences are new opportunities which appear in order to help you reach your destination in a roundabout way. You always decide according to your free will. On Earth this applies: your free will aids you in decision-making, and should also be respected by the spiritual world.

To live the life purpose, to implement and live the related fields of learning, which you had set yourselves as the main topic, besides many small challenges, means fulfilment for the life of the soul. Every spark of light aspires to the completion of the learning areas. It can then leave the Earth (die) fulfilled and in peace.

The temptations of life, being kept away from your true path, should be accepted. Such is life!

The free will on Earth wishes to be tested and trained in the material world. It wants to be seen and respected, because it is a means of setting boundaries where necessary. Your will mobilizes the mind and the body, it belongs to you and should be caringly appreciated. It has its duty.

Your will helps you to change thought into matter.

In Harry Potter books it says: materialize; making something which exists only energetically, visible to the eye. Or turning something which you need and want to work on, into matter. Establishing vibrations in your material world was a challenge to many cultures. Turning thoughts and ideas into matter, making them visible and tangible, is an illusion. On your Earth you deal with solids. Light energy, vibrations of light, are mainly invisible to you people and therefore non-existent. What you can see and touch is real.

Images, visualisations, and ideas are invisible, therefore they do not exist.

They exist only as vibration, as energy.

Materializing is a way of making the invisible visible, i.e. turning it into matter.

Many shamans mastered this technique more or less.

At present, in your era, just before the awakening of consciousness, with divine help, I wish to instruct you on this.

It is an experience which can raise everybody's consciousness.

The belief that only what I see exists is hereby repealed.

The invisible, too, exists and is real. It can be seen and felt materially. Starting with our thoughts: Every thought is normally invisible. You say thoughts are free.

Basically, the free will can create and send out thoughts liberally. Thoughts are energy waves which come into motion by thought. A thought is information brought into vibration. A vibration is always movement.

Some thoughts are directed at specific people. There are thoughts directed at nothing in particular, into the unknown, or thoughts directed at an object, and many more.

Your everyday life points out the countless diversity of thought. A thought is energy which, once sent out, generally reaches the person it was intended for – much like a letter which is sent and arrives at the addressee. In your fast-moving everyday life, your thinking is often uncontrolled because you think a lot and you think very fast. You are exposed to a variety of information and rarely filter out details. Often someone thinks, 'oh, how come I am thinking of so or so?' This means having been 'thought of'.

If the thought is positively controlled, it is pleasing, conversely it produces discomfort for which there is no apparent reason.

When similar thoughts accumulate e.g. regarding the weather, it occurs as was thought about. You can think about and create a weather condition. During the holidays, many people think, 'no bad weather, please' or 'please, it must not rain'. The energetic statement is, 'bad weather, please' and 'it may rain'.

The particle *not* is incomprehensible in the energy realm. It is regarded as a filler word (such as: er, um, ah, ...). *Not, no* and *none* are neutral in the spiritual energy field.

When many people have thoughts regarding the weather, a wave of energy is created, and manifests as rain and bad weather during the holidays.

Thus (uncontrolled) thoughts quickly result in something which we encounter in life directly. Thoughts have been manifested.

Many wishes and ideas can be manifested!

Example:

When I have a good, specific idea, I think it over and over again, and it does not go out of my head. If I deal with it, I evaluate and analyse it. If I find it really good and it inspires and enthuses me, then the thought with the information of the idea enters my heart.

I start loving the idea. This love for the idea becomes really strong, and my will is roused. It wishes to take the idea realising that it is a heartfelt desire. Such an amount of loving thought over an extended period, together with the confidence of implementing it, plus the support of the will, makes the idea visible after a certain time. Now something tangible has resulted from the thought. I have materialized something.

In the new era, with the light vibration, these scenarios take place faster, and with the heart energy, the thoughts create themselves.

Please control your thoughts. Think positively for the benefit of all people, animals, plants, Mother Earth and all that exists.

Positive thoughts vibrate at a higher level and delight everyone.

Positive thoughts heal wounds and injuries.

Positive thoughts manifest themselves favourably in your environment.

Positive thoughts shape your New Earth, so think them!

Your life today is very colourful, there are lots of influences, media, many kinds of distractions.

You are mobile and travel the world, for business, or for pleasure to amuse yourselves. These are the games of distraction which you play with yourselves. You want to see and experience everything. Today you know a lot about your Earth, which was unimaginable in earlier times. You have realised many visions today in order to explore your exterior world.

Do you also know yourself?

Do you know who you are, or are you running away from yourselves?

In silence, stillness and meditation you can identify and explore yourselves: who you really are, what your wishes are, what your soul wants. When you encounter yourselves in the silence, you change and begin to recognise external influences as distractions. To recognise and study oneself creates reliability and confidence. You accept yourselves with all your problems and worries, but also with all your joys and visions. You expand your consciousness and sense your own *value*. Learn to appreciate yourselves and discover the strengths (treasures) within you. The exterior world loses its appeal. Your inner strength leads you to your life purpose, to clarity and purity.

You stabilize your inner values and live them. The goals you have visualised are significant and wish to be realised. The individual is occupied with itself, with its life. Looking at and comparing yourself with others becomes unimportant; you are too busy with yourself.

Only when you have researched and understood yourself, you can understand and help others.

Only when you have accomplished your mission in life and have dealt with all your learning fields, will you be free.

Only when you have understood the interaction of the soul with the body, can you heal.

Only when you are spiritually awakened, will you understand the interrelationships of your world, life and death.

The same is true for shaping one's own life, and life can be lived this way too.

It deeply satisfies the soul.

I Am the divine vibration of Christ in the form of Maitreya,
I raise your physical vibration with my channelled texts.
I guide you in divine joy and divine love.

Tsakpo, an incarnate master, evokes the beauty of planet Earth

I Am the Light vibration Tsakpo. I wish to touch your hearts and open them to the beauty of your terrestrial world.

Not so long ago, I lived on your beautiful planet and was able to have the experiences you are now undergoing. The earthly insights and the emotional experiences touched and delighted me profoundly. I feel for you!

You are children of heaven and Earth, united in your body.

Absorb the energy of the Earth and of heaven. This boosts your spirit and makes your heart vibrate.

Run barefoot through grass or sand, swim in your oceans, or let your feet bathe in spring water. This strengthens your root chakra (energy vortex in the lower pelvic area) and clarifies your actions and creations. Honour Mother Earth, she deserves it. She carries you and your home, nourishes your fruit, swallows your garbage and many pollutants which you have created. Dancing on the Earth, on the dusty sand, on the grass, chanting 'Tare, Tare, Om Tare Tuttare Ture Soham' honours the Great Mother and elates her. A joyous Mother Earth nourishes your fruit optimally and happily supports you too. In her joy she forgives everything. Please honour the Great Gaia and sympathise with her.

Dancing and chanting aligns you consciously with the Earth, and you communicate with her and this pleases her greatly. Many indigenous peoples have recognised this and have always done so. These are important rituals to honour the Earth. Your harvest festivals are ancient pagan festivals in which, in former times already, Earth was thanked for her gifts. Giving thanks is a sacred energy, which Mother Earth too needs to heal.

The sky, the universe, nourishes you with light vibrations, which are felt strongly in a bright starry sky and a full moon.

Weather permitting, sleep in the open air and connect yourselves with the universe and the Divine Being within you by 'looking at the sky'. This beautiful night sky supplies the systems of your body with tranquillity and deep peace. The nervous system can be balanced and healed by the celestial energy. The full moon energy strengthens your femininity. Men too have female aspects, and these are balanced. The full moon assists women to gain their female power. Place a glass of water at the window on full moon nights, and let the moon energize the water. The next morning, it can be drunk. It stabilizes the hormonal balance in men and women, helps to get through menopause harmoniously, can realise the desire to have children, and supports women in their feminine power.

The celestial energy brings a lot of divine light into your body and expands consciousness. The raising of consciousness is needed in the time to come, for your Earth is transforming. The Earth will be more flooded with light, and thus everything living on Earth, even mankind. An expanded consciousness helps understand these processes and participate in the transformation. Your consciousness expands when you allow the celestial light to flow into your body through the crown chakra (the energy vortex on top of your head). Understanding who you are, helps you.

The soul which inhabits your body feeds on the divine light of the universe. Your body needs the energy of the Earth to live and to create/ to act.

Both energies feed you, and unite in your heart. This heart energy expands your consciousness and radiates from you and around you. The energy of the heart chakra (the energy vortex at your heart) is the life energy available to you.

When both these energy vortices, the root and heart chakras, are active and absorb the energy from the universe and the Earth, they unite in the heart giving the body the power to create life consciously. When one, or both, of these chakras is inactive, the person has little vitality and is energetically 'undernourished'.

Healers or people with knowledge concerning these energy gates can be helpful in such cases, and balance the energy gates.

The wind, the sun, the water and the Earth have worked together as a unit for many eons, and have shaped your world. Now, in your era, they prepare the Earth for the transition onto the higher vibrational level. As a unit only have they mastered all the transformations of the Earth over many periods of time, and so too will it be this time.

The sun is already sending the results of its transformation to the galaxy. The sun changes through immense, unimaginable energies resulting from explosions, and it discards ballast which it transforms itself through the direct combustion. This energetic process of combustion on the sun unleashes hot winds (extremely fast moving energy) which will also reach the Earth. Over many years, the winds cool off on their way through the galaxy, but are still warm when reaching the Earth.

The oceans rejoice over these warm winds, and in turn, they can set the cleansing process in motion. The heat of these winds causes movement in the oceans, and they purify themselves. They expand and inspire the rivers and lakes to participate in this process. Land is flooded, entire rivers change their courses, and new land emerges from the sea.

This period of transformation is imminent, it is predetermined and is already active in the galaxy.

Mankind will spend this period in a deep peaceful state resembling sleep, and will emerge feeling strengthened and energetically elated.

These changes have been planned, and hosts of divine spiritual guides from the Central Sun will lead and guide this process.

Every human being will be raised according to their life plan and will be in their designated position. Simply trust, everything will happen the way it should according to the divine plan!

Your animals and plants will be supported by the helpers of their divine world and gently guided through the changes. The animals too will be in a state of peace, which will heal them and permeate their cells with light. They will awake, as will you, in a new state of consciousness.

It is inappropriate to worry or even make arrangements for the period of transition. The divine hosts of angels and helpers are already under way to direct and guide you.

To understand the elevation of the Earth is a challenge, but it is inscrutable!

Free yourselves from the idea that you could provide for the time of transition.

Father-Mother God themselves protect and guide the Earth into the higher dimension.

Just trust!

Your peace and serenity prepare and guide you.

Your light-filled body needs to be nourished and supported during the ascension process.

Now already, your cells are lighter than they were three years ago. The increased light photons of the etherial layer of Earth radiate into the cells of your body and slowly but surely change your body system. Sometimes you notice this by the changing sleep-wake rhythm, or the desire to spend some time at the sea/in the mountains, or you notice new food preferences, or you need more time for yourself in peace and quiet, etc. Many things are possible.

These are often only trivialities – observe yourself.

Eating habits will change inadvertently because the body is adapting the digestive tract. The light cells of your body also need lighter nourishment to feed on. It will be very noticeable that you will only need a little food. The number of meals and the amount of food intake will be greatly reduced. Many will be concerned, 'Why do I eat so little?' Your body will take the energy from the sunlight, which is enriched with photons. And also the food is to supply the body with more light. Food with a lower vibration (light-reduced food) will be experienced as being indigestible.

Your cells need light to sustain a healthy body. All herbs have stored a large amount of light, and are consequently well tolerated by the body. Many vegetables are similarly permeated with light. The body needs root vegetables and similar crops to strengthen its connection to the Earth. Fruit and nuts have already stored the increased light, and are very good for the body as a staple food. All animal products are difficult to digest because the animal cells, like those of the humans, must be raised, and it will take some time before the animal cells are able to store this light in them. Consequently, with the animal products, you are feeding your body's old cell system. Of course, these products can be eaten and are not dangerous for the body. Only light food, and really only light food, changes your body towards a light-filled system.

Each one of you should sense what is good for you, and what not.

The intake of food is a subjective attitude because each person vibrates at a different frequency. Take responsibility for your own body; it will reward you with well-being, radiance, and health.

The water you drink cleanses your body and carries information.

If you want to supply your body with good, healing water, this should be individually programmed to attain the desired effect.

Water can be programmed because it has a consciousness, it is intelligent. In a glass, water can be influence or charged using sound, texts, symbols, colours, songs, places of power on images, photos, and many more. Water can re-programme itself, can restructure its molecules assuming the desired vibration for your glass of water. This allows simple tap water to become healing water. The knowledge of programming water was discovered in the 1980s by a Japanese, Masaru Emoto, and published in his book. Read it up so you can understand that water has a consciousness and is communicative. A prayer directed at the consciousness of water creates healing water.

And how do you programme healing water for yourselves?

All options listed may be applied. The water can be spoken or sung to, exposed to music, a picture can be held to or placed under the glass, a symbol placed in or next to the glass can cause the molecules to change. Gems can also program water very well. The consciousness of the water communicates with the consciousness of the gemstone.

Crystals and gemstones have very different colours and shapes.

The tasks and intelligence of the stones differ too. Please accept the statement that every stone has a consciousness and carries specific information. The stone gladly reveals this information, however, the communication is somewhat difficult - or it is not. You can access this knowledge and programme water by placing the stone into it. The stone passes its information to the water and you can absorb it physically.

Your cells then bear the information of the stone and apply its wisdom physically.

There are healers, shamans and professionals who understand the power and healing properties of stones. For eons, gemstones and crystals have carried knowledge in them. They developed 'at snail's pace' and are truly as old as the hills. The colours of crystals have a significance. The radiation of each colour affects our body system. Colours are vibrations containing high light frequencies and information. Humans react very differently to colours, which illustrates your individuality. You say: Everyone has their particular preferences, and so it is. This statement applies to all areas of life.

This statement regarding individuals can also be applied to stones.

Colour, shape, type and location of each stone/crystal is as particular as every human being. Stones and also our water have a consciousness. Water can be programmed, and, consequently, so can stones.

A crystal can be programmed by yourself, for yourself.

Example:

You have a beautiful rock crystal and would like it to be your guardian stone.

Say a prayer and connect to the divine energy. Place the stone in your left hand and talk to it. Tell it what purpose it is to serve, and ask it to assume this function. Remain silent and in the grace of God. Then bless the stone and touch it with your love (mentally). Thank the stone for assuming the desired assignment. Thank the divine energies as well, and trust your programming. The stone is now charged specifically for you.

Placed in water, it can also heal your body.

Try it!

This is how energies cooperate with your consciousness, or with the consciousness of water, stones, plants, Mother Earth, and other planets.

Your everyday life seems dull and monotonous.

Due to the daily lack of variety and the occupational stupidity you resemble robots. My goodness, is it not you who creates your life, who chose your job, who built this house, who married your spouse, who always flies to the Maldives on holiday - and now you complain that life is a routine and is boring?

Keep complaining. Nothing will change unless you do something about it. Each person is responsible for their body (as mentioned), but also for their life. Every day you may say, 'Something has to change', but that does not change anything.

Each individual alone can and should shape and change their life. The more rituals you have in your everyday life, including holidaying in the same place, the less variety you have. Life is relatively undeviating.

Do something different. Change the route to work, the evening entertainment at home, your holiday, etc. Take responsibility for yourself and for your life, be creative. Do you still have visions and dreams for your life? Look at them and work on the implementation of these desires. You can also change your occupation if you have the courage and the ideas to that effect.

My goodness ..., do enjoy your life and live actively until you reach old age. Goals lend life new impetus, which penetrates every cell of your body. Starting new projects, perhaps together with your partner or with friends, enriches everyday life.

It is important to joyfully organise your daily life, and thus your entire life.

Experiencing joy on all levels of being creates satisfaction and happiness. Those who are happy live in peace with themselves and others.

However, there are many people who complain about having a hectic life.

Here too, things need to be changed, whining and complaining are inappropriate. You have created this yourself. Analyse your day and find out what causes your stress.

Ask yourself, who or what you are running after. Who or what is pushing you?

Maybe you want to achieve something special? Is it worth pushing yourself?

Maybe you want to prove something to yourself or to others?

Maybe you take on too much because you cannot say 'no'?

Maybe you should delegate more?

Recognise the problem and change the situation; your personal happiness is at stake. Being in harmony with oneself and with life is beneficial for all areas of life.

Please be aware that you are the creator of your life, you are the responsible one.

Create your life as you have always imagined it to be - joyful.

Recognise the value of your own life!

With all my heart
and in universal love
this is what I wish for each of you.
Greetings from Tsakpo

Lady Portia, the transparent light vibration

I Am Lady Portia, the master of the transformative process which is now destined for Earth.

With deep joy and divine love, I guide you through this energetic text, which is to bring knowledge and is to clarify you.

I am the I AM presence of your new era; I accompany you in peace and harmony.

Pass through my gate of consciousness and awaken to life anew.

Your Earth wishes to change.

It is predetermined and has been known for eons that an earthly cycle is now complete.

Now, right now, you are in the middle of this process of change of which everybody writes and talks, and yet it is so hard for you to understand.

Until now, you could have the most wonderful experiences on your planet. The light and the dark sides of your galaxy lived on Earth side by side. Lots of things, almost everything on your Earth was possible. Both the low and the high energies manifested and appeared in the form of humans, animals, situations, and in the many wars and battles which you were able to fight here. Now the old patterns of behaviour on Earth are changing.

Across the world, your energy/vibration has been increasing constantly but steadily since 1945. Now, the process is faster. The light energies have been accelerated thus tearing down the old structures of the Earth. The energy is being converted into an energy of peace on Earth.

The middle, your former harmony, is the stabilisation of the oscillation between the two energy poles.

In the middle, both poles have the same energy component. It is neutral.

Your current energy strives towards this middle and wants to overcome it. Thus, the energy of the low-vibrating pole is reduced. You then live in the prevailing energy of the pole vibrating at a higher energy level. This changes your life. Your thinking and feeling takes place in higher energies. For you, this means the lower energies vanish from the way you think and feel. Your thinking is filled with light, you think at a high level of vibration. The lower thoughts are unfathomable; they are behind the middle on the linear ray and are marginalized by overcoming the centre.

**This diagram shows the energy ray of the Earth
(an image for the mind).**

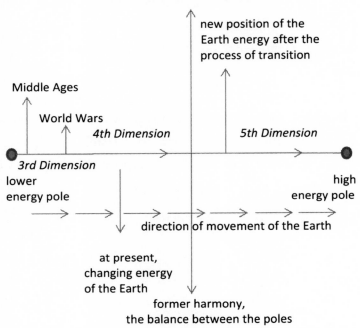

the position between the poles

new position of the
Earth energy after the
process of transition

Middle Ages

World Wars

4th Dimension

5th Dimension

3rd Dimension

lower
energy pole

high
energy pole

direction of movement of the Earth

at present,
changing energy
of the Earth

former harmony,
the balance between the poles

The diagram addresses your intellect, which can visually see what is happening in the upcoming dimensional shift. It is only a change in energy. The Earth moves, it moves on to a different energy level. It happens exactly as shown in the diagram.

The 3rd Dimension is the old era in which you lived and were able to gain experience.

The 4th Dimension lies between the third and fifth dimensions. It lies between two fictitious poles and is very mobile. Unfortunately you cannot exist in this state forever because of the constant movement, the instability, the inconsistency of the two poles. The 5th Dimension offers you energetic living conditions in a higher, balanced energy once more.

The linear energy ray illustrates where you lived, what energy prevailed there, and why it was possible that there were battles/wars with all kinds of atrocities. It was the predominant low energy, which made this possible. All incarnated souls at that time had chosen this era; they had included the fighting and atrocities in their soul plan in order to experience them.

At this crucial point at which the Earth now is, overcoming the middle, the 4th Dimension, in order to be renewed and fit for life in the 5th Dimension, it is a challenge for many souls who want to witness this. Therefore, Earth is so overpopulated, many incarnations are taking place because the transformation of Earth is an experience not to be missed.

The Earth is now moving to the middle (the 4th Dimension). Many people are already in the 4th Dimension regarding their body vibration, and feel that life is fast and hectic, almost confusing. The 4th Dimension, the transitional phase, is energetically very unstable, a kind of 'sorting place'.

Once you have reached the 5th Dimension, everything will 'feel' slower and calmer. The day will be longer. Once the transformation is complete, you will find your equilibrium. After the transitional phase all body systems will calm down again and be healed by the light.

It is important to leave old upsetting thoughts and deeds behind in the old energy, in peace. They can stay there because that is where they belong. In the high energy they are useless. They weigh you down heavily and energetically keep you fixed in the 3ʳᵈ Dimension.

Please read this text nonjudgmentally. Judging and criticising also belong in the third Dimension, so just let go of it.

Be aware now, right now, that you can experience everything in all three dimensions, but only now.

Old patterns, thought patterns, behavioural patterns and physical patterns remain in the 3ʳᵈ Dimension, RELEASE THEM. The past with all its experiences belongs to the old structure. Just rid yourself of it. Is important for you to recognise that the old patterns were good, but are now unusable and should, with lots of love, be left behind, where they originated.

The 'middle' of the diagram is about experiencing change. When living in the middle, sense the unrest between the two energy poles: a lingering in the 'old', and the feeling of being attracted to the new. Your thoughts and actions undergo a change in direction which is unfamiliar to you. It is a challenge to pluck up the courage to abandon yourself to the attraction of the new energy.

To live in the pole of light, in the 5ᵗʰ Dimension, to stay and live there makes life easier and is liberating. A complete transition into the energy of Light requires that you be clarified, which is difficult because most living conditions are still in the 3ʳᵈ and 4ᵗʰ Dimensions. Thus all the souls living on Earth now have the unique opportunity of being able to feel and experience three dimensions. Only the transition between these dimensions teaches and strengthens you to make a decision. Each of you can choose a dimension freely where you can live and create. Each of you, young or old, may quite individually decide where they want to spend their lives, and with which energy vibrations they want to experience their learning processes.

The time in which you live is a time of transition into another dimension.

The energy ray of the diagram can be applied to all areas of life. You can name the poles light and darkness, or good and evil.

Based on the diagram, it is possible to reflect and see where you find yourself presently.

The entire planet including all the systems is in this process of change: the Earth itself, the oceans, nature, every person, politics, the economic systems, simply everything. The body systems are also integrated into these processes and are required to enlighten and heal themselves, or to take the decision to remain in the old energy and experience everything once more. All of you, everybody, is free to decide for themselves.

So be it!

It is necessary to describe how the universe, the Divine Energy, Father-Mother God created themselves.

You speak of God, the Father Almighty. These are images from the 3rd Dimension and were helpful for many generations. These images originated in the religions with spiritual help. Personifying God the

Father was the vision of the old era. It was easy to convey authority and punishment, rules of life were enforced by churches. Religion assumed the authority of God. The churches served as mediators.

A liberal recognition of laws would have been unthinkable; it would have been undermined by brute force.

Buddhism, the religious images of natives, and the Indian deities were more liberal. In these religious persuasions, individuals were already more responsible for themselves.

The God-Father image portrayed God as a punishing God; and instead of the people being responsible to the Divine, the Church assumed this responsibility. The believers obeyed the Church and its interpretations of the Divine voice. Dependencies incurred, whereby the Church became a domain of power.

This mistake of the past is put into perspective by the energies of Light.

The systems of the church are flooded with light, crimes are discovered, power structures are revealed. Your churches fall silent when answers relative to the new era are sought. Questions pertaining to the time of transition remain unanswered by the churches. People in powerful clerical positions speak against the Light, calling it unrealistic and fictitious. The Church (still) rejects transparency, the risk of being 'seen through' is too great. Of course, there are many people working in your churches who truly mean well. The implementation of truthfulness by the church authorities is still very limited. The support of the Church in recognizing the structures seems to be calculated.

Make your own picture, consider, and look attentively.

The light vibrations penetrate all earthly machinations.

Each person should experience, see and understand the image of God as flooded with light.

The Divine Energy is the highest energy in all universes, inconceivable to the mind. Believing, trusting in the Divine Energy, depends on every human being.

We need to take responsibility for our own faith and to establish trust in the Divine.

Who is the Creator?

What is mankind?

This knowledge is released by the vibration of light.

You have already received the definition of mankind. You know that the body houses the soul. The soul is immortal and its home is in the Divine, it is the spark of God. It is regarded as a spin-off from the Divine, the Great Almighty Light. If this is so, you have, being a spark of God, the same power and energy, the creative force, as the Almighty One. Only with regard to the spark. You know the saying, both on the large and the small scale. This statement applies and should be heeded.

The divine omnipotence has the incredible power of creating entire universes and directing all that is.

You call it creating, for God is the Creator of all that *IS*. The word 'creating' carries the message: create with intelligence, creating creatively for the benefit of all.

The incredible intelligence of God Almighty can create all that is.

Confer this statement to the divine spark within you. In this way, applying its inherent intelligence to the environment, the soul can create and design. With great respect to the sacred Divine Energy, every soul is the creator of its own world, its life. The process of incarnation allows you, as embodied souls, to create your own life according to the Divine image.

You humans are creators of your lives, of the learning areas, and of the world around you.

The high level of responsibility inherent in this statement is to be considered calmly.

The Divine energy of the 'One-in-All' is in each of you. You all possess the same charisma and intelligence as the Divine with regard to the unity of your soul. Accept your intelligence, be aware of your power, and begin to create.

Your life is in your hands, take responsibility for yourself.

This insight is an expansion of consciousness of the 5th Dimension.

To manifest this knowledge in your cells and to establish it in your consciousness, this affirmation will help:

I and the Creator are one.
> or

I create my life.
> or

I am the spark of God.

These very simplified images of the Almighty Creator are presented to you in His name so you can understand.

The unfathomable greatness of the Divine Power cannot be described in words.

With the blessing of God the Almighty
Lady Portia takes her leave.

14

Jesus Christ, divine love
and human suffering

*I Am Christ, the Son of God, ascended into heaven seated at the
right hand of God the Father.*
*I want to intensify the love among you and put an end to the
suffering on Earth.*

Love among you people in the 3rd Dimension is often understood as physical
contact and is lived as such. Love involves opening the heart at all levels.

The physical level is your tool, which of course should be permeated
with the energy of love.

The spiritual level understands and lives love universally, energetically.

The soul level needs love as nourishment on Earth.

Love, flowing from the heart, is energy of a high frequency and has
healing powers. This high, healing vibration is a cooperation of the

divine celestial energy and the Earth energy, which unite in the heart chakra of a human being. A conscious person with spiritual knowledge can control and direct both these energies.

You think this is the privilege of healers. With the knowledge of this technique, each of you has the ability, and can heal.

Using your hands, words and spiritual contact, healing can take place with the help of the energies of the Earth and the energies of heaven. Both energies united form the love that flows from your heart.

The heart is the divine organ of the body; it is the engine that drives the body and thus your life in a human body. Many cardiac diseases suggest an insufficient energy supply to the heart. Our native Earth energy flows through the root chakra, and the universal, Divine Light through the crown chakra. Only the combination of both energies in the heart can strengthen the heart and keep it healthy. Lacking one of these energies or a failed merger can cause damage to the heart on the energetic level. Awareness hereof can already effect healing. Open both these chakras to feel the full force of life, and grant your heart the love it needs. Of course, all the chakras of the body should be clear and well activated. This alone strengthens your physical health.

The energy of love is your human creative potential to express yourselves and to create. 'Love can move mountains', as the saying goes. That is true.

With the energy of love, which is fed by the Earth and the universe you can work miracles.

Focussed and consciously used, it is *the* healing energy (the Divine Energy meets the Earth energy) which is available to you as human beings. Radiated from your hands, it is also called prana. Do you now understand my work on Earth? As Jesus on Earth, touching with my hands brought healing.

Many healers and spiritually conscious people are aware of the force of the heart energy, the energy of love.

It is accessible to everyone because you all have the ability to use this vibration of love. In the new era, the knowledge pertaining to the energy of love will be easier to implement and will be commonly used as healing power.

All people on Earth are created according to the same pattern: an earthly body, animated by a spark of light, the soul. The outward appearance of a body, size, skin colour, gender, etc. are unimportant. The soul is what gives the body its specific charisma, what makes us human.

The incarnated souls have different stages of development: there are quite fresh, new souls, young souls, aged souls, old souls, matured souls, mature souls, and master souls. At present, very many intergalactic souls are coming to Earth. Depending on the maturity of the soul, the learning areas have been chosen for this life. Hence every human being is very specific – identical people can hardly be found. A wonderful variety, and yet you are all equal. You are composed of the same ingredients. You are *one* and yet *different*.

You wage battles and wars even though you are brothers and sisters. You generate suffering with low energy, such as envy, jealousy, hatred, greed, lust for power, and so on. The suffering on Earth has created great karma and has held you in captivity for many lifetimes of suffering. Every life on Earth has had to endure suffering, sorrow and grief. Therefore souls often experienced rebirth as being difficult, having to descend into the lower energies and to live in a material body.

When ascending through the 4th into the 5th Dimension, you will leave the suffering behind you. You slip it off like a shirt. The shirt remains in the 3rd Dimension where the experiences of suffering are housed. This rejection of suffering frees you, sets you free for new possibilities of creation.

The experiences awaiting you in the new era all have a liberal energy.

Internalise this idea → FREEDOM – thereby free from suffering – therefore carefree.

To attain this knowledge makes the ascent into the higher vibration worthwhile. In the 5th Dimension, where only transparent energies vibrate, you will recognize the machinations which create suffering. With this knowledge and with the new energy, generating suffering is impossible. During the process of recognition, these low vibrations will be seen through and transformed. In the 5th Dimension, the contamination by low frequencies will be impossible since they will already have been transformed during the process of recognition. While reading this, please allow yourself to be guided by an unbiased attitude.

Now sense the difference in the energy of the 3rd and the 5th Dimensions; sense it in speaking and in thinking, thus also in your actions.

In the 4th Dimension the cleansing power of knowledge dominates. Here the difference between the other two dimensions becomes clear. The 4th Dimension unveils everything. Many processes on Earth are currently in this dimension for they are being seen through.

From this 4th Dimension, the level of determination, you can return to the 3rd Dimension or advance to the 5th. The choice is yours – at all times. Each of your decisions will be accepted by the divine spiritual world.

This great decision, this transformation at present, makes everything so exciting on planet Earth and in the entire galaxy for all souls and even the spiritual world.

Read this text several times. It contains energies of the 5th Dimension which transform cognizance of events into knowledge.

The energy and the knowledge of this ascension process into the 5th Dimension were contained in the messages of your bibles concerning the person of Jesus Christ, then already. In spite of the adulteration of these texts over a thousand years, the original essence has been preserved.

We now find ourselves in this 'special time' which, however, already took place many times in other galaxies. For these are recurring universal expansion processes of our entire universe.

May my message remain with you,
today and in the future,
in eternal love to the Divine,
in the Christ Energy, I AM.

Master Confucius explains the future areas of learning

I greet you. I, Master Confucius, am speaking to you.
I would like to inform you about the new learning areas on your
planet Earth.

The children living with you on Earth now, and also those who will be born in the next few years, are the children of Light. They live on and come from the radiant stellar systems and have agreed to participate in the ascension of the earth into the 5th Dimension.

Rejoice over these luminous souls in child form. They are mature, wise souls who have assumed their mission on this planet and are playing their part on behalf of the entire galaxy. The children of the new era from the radiant spheres are not yet understood and accepted by society, they are not recognised in their mission as helpers of the galaxy. This text is to make you understand why these souls are so important for the Earth and for the knowledge of interconnections of the universe.

I, Master Confucius, entreat you people on Earth to welcome your children with love, with the high frequency of universal light, for love is the elixir for you on the planet. Do understand that these souls spring from pure love and *are* pure love. You call the children of the New Age crystal children and also have other names for them. But you need to understand this: naming is only an exterior act. These children feed on the frequency of love from their parents, grandparents, and people in their immediate vicinity, in kindergarten, school, etc. The quality of their lives depends on the quality of light in their environment.

What is important NOW is the realisation and awareness of how these children should grow up in order to live in their own perfect quality of light and to spread this light on Earth.

There are many different models in every culture. Every country works on its own philosophy of how children and adolescents should grow up. You try out many things, but are unable to assess the background and implications of your actions.

The children need parental love. It is a necessity of life. It is the food of the subtle body. It is vitally important. Furthermore, the basis for the perfect development of your children is the issue of trust, and the possibility to develop freely on all levels. This trust can only be met when the adults are aware of their children's origin, respect and promote this knowledge. A child with a luminous soul is to be guided gently and be taught about life in the material world because it needs helps to orient itself on Earth.

Trust the individual abilities of these children, for through loving interaction these abilities will develop fully. A liberal upbringing and a relaxed way of dealing with the children ensures the individual development which is necessary. It lends stability to the identification and dedication needed for the specific life tasks of the souls. Only by way of loving guidance can the soul of a child attain its individual tasks.

For many children life in the material world (on Earth) is foreign. They had not previously lived on Earth.

Parents of such luminous children, heed my words and have the courage to get involved with your children. The consciousness of these souls from the stellar galaxies is very high. Power games and battles are alien to them.

Your teaching systems should adapt speedily to accommodate the scholastic needs of the stellar children of Light. These children bear the knowledge of universal energy, correlations, and possibilities within themselves. You need only promote and unlock it, and the blossoming of all capabilities will be secured.

During the first years of life, life in the material world, on Earth, can be explained and exemplified to the children. Caging them in and limiting them are inappropriate. Gentle guidance and loving devotion are the easiest methods for a beneficial development.

We, the Ascended Masters, assist all people who are responsible for the development of new teaching systems. May they attain conscious knowledge on the promotion of children – speedily.

The main responsibility lies with the parents. The loving care in the parental home is irreplaceable.

Look at the dolphins and other animal species which have a high consciousness. There the entire group (the extended family) is responsible for rearing the young.

In the western countries, families living together are usually small, and in the materially weaker countries on your planet, families are large. The richer countries often prefer educational models in which children are guided and shaped into efficient and adjusted adults, who then take their place in the achievement-oriented society and make their contribution towards society for the benefit of money.

In the poorer regions, children grow up being free, but are responsible for their survival at a young age already.

They earn their livelihood with poorly paid activities, and often have to help feed their families.

Both models are illiberal forms of shaping the children of light in the new era and should be changed for the sake of your Earth.

Western selfishness causes this lack of freedom to arise and turns children into the property of adults.

For the future of your planet, these selfish machinations are to be transformed into liberal creativity. Acceptance and devotion are the most supportive measures for your stellar children. Be aware, you adults, the future of your planet lies in the hands of these incarnated stellar souls.

In great awareness of all the necessary changes on Earth, in God's name, I,
Confucius, offer my help unstintingly to all incarnated souls.
I greet you in the Eternal Light.
Master Confucius

Lady Aurora has accompanied Earth since its inception

I greet you, dear children on Earth, on Gaia, the mother soul.
I am Aurora, the master of old.
From the inception of the Earth, I have supported its development
with my pink-ruby energy ray. In this current new era, my white-
golden energy ray emerges to assist mankind during this time of
transition into the 5th Dimension.

Since the dawn of time your planet Earth has experienced many processes of change.

Many residents from other galaxies have experimented on Earth causing great changes. Now, the experimentation is over, the Earth is ascending onto the next level of vibration. This is a birth into the new light energy extending over a longer period of time (from your view). All areas of your life are affected by the rise in energy; no one can escape this. You ascend collectively. For you people the increased energy will be experienced as a rise in consciousness. Your thinking and feeling is *different*. Your environment is changing in that houses, factories, forests, and vast areas of land disappear or are rebuilt and restructured. Of course there have always been changes on Earth, but now the changes are massive, and you experience them consciously. You see them with eyes energetically renewed. The environment, the entire Earth adapts to the new energy of the 5th Dimension.

How does this take place?

Your Earth, Mother Earth, is a great soul with an immensely high consciousness. She too will increase her consciousness. This increase in consciousness is preceded by a cleansing at all levels. This cleansing process is currently being effected on Earth and will span twenty to thirty years.

The inner turmoil is experienced in the form of earthquakes or volcanic eruptions. The Earth renews itself from the core outward.

The breathing of Mother Earth is seen in the tides and the geysers, and the coughing, the expulsion of toxins from the Earth, takes place in the form of volcanic eruptions.

The Earth is alive and thus subject to cleansing processses, as is your body.

The oceans will change and flood vast areas. New land will be exposed elsewhere. The water purifies and renews the land. The coastal regions should remain uninhabited. If necessary, resettlements should take place.

The time frame for this purification comprises about ten years and will start gradually so that mankind will be able to act timeously, provided you consider the expansion of the oceans when developing residential areas.

Mother Earth shows the changes taking place and you can understand them all.

Be wise and take the signs seriously.

Some of you can communicate with Mother Earth.

Please speak to the great soul; it will warn you and predict when the expiration or the water purification starts, and which areas will be affected. It is important to Mother Earth that you understand her reactions, for they are indispensable. She wants to illustrate the inevitability of her natural processes and hereby make them intelligible.

Please communicate with her!

The Great Mother does not intend to inflict harm on her children. The conscious earth-soul cares for each of you - for the human race, the animals, the plants, and all the minerals. It is the basis of all life in and on it. Mother Earth desires that life on and in her be heaven on Earth.

Prior to your civilisation, many indigenous people recognized the Great Soul, Earth, and were in constant contact with it. Then, the contact between the medicine men and the Great Mother was intense. I am attempting to revive your understanding of the wisdom and of the elevated consciousness of the Earth because, for your future on Earth, the contact, the communication with Mother Gaia, is of great importance for you and for your planet. It will be unthinkable in the future to live *apart* from Gaia, energetically, as you do now. Being *a part* of her is the only option you have (as *part*ners). Be aware of the Great Holy Soul of Earth and of the knowledge it possesses since the dawn of creation.

If, in your heart, you understand who and what the Earth is, the pollution you inflict upon it is insane. Only through the love in your heart can you, children of mankind, experience and thus understand the nature of Earth and the importance it has for your lives.

What matters to me is that you finally understand what and who the Great Holy Mother Earth is. She lives, she feels, she is aware of all experiences and knows mankind from the dawn of time.

Mother Earth, in her infinite benevolence, bears and nourishes you children of Earth and wants to continue doing so. Do understand her desire to purge herself. Accept the purification of the Earth with all its consequences and give it your blessing. This process is inevitable: The Earth wants to rid itself from the waste of the past billion years and be filled with light, ready for the 5th Dimension.

It is the same process your human body is undergoing.

Being aware of the necessary clarification of the Earth, contact with the Great Soul should be sought. The Great Mother is ready to communicate with you for it will give her great pleasure. Thus pending changes regarding the water and land masses can become known timeously, and human lives can be spared owing to this information. The contact between mankind and the planet is supported and promoted by the spiritual world. This also helps you raise your consciousness. To express gratitude to your planet, meditations and rituals are the easiest means of communication available to you.

Remember the rituals of the indigenous people; they were aware of the high consciousness of their planet Earth, respected it, and held it in high esteem. This show of respect should be continued, in gratitude and great humility.

Only then will the Earth be able to feed and heal you, the animals and everything it bears. Your planet has a strong healing power; everything on Earth (plants, stones, organic material, water) can be cured by the energy of Earth. You simply need to establish contact and gratefully accept the healing, consciously.

In the future, this is the new, albeit an old healing method; it only requires the awareness that the Earth is alive, that it is and always has been a great holy soul.

Today already you heal with herbs, stones and mud, water and mineral substances; all this is terrestrial, everything comes from the Mother. In the near future you will not need the detour via the plants, rocks and minerals.

The contact in spirit, from human soul to Earth soul, with the awareness of healing, will effect healing at the body level.

Therefore, the human connection to Mother Earth is so crucial for the future.

The Earth rises into the fifth Dimension; this energy increase is inevitable and is sealed by the galactic council of your solar system.

You can ascend with the Earth if – due to an increased awareness – you so decide. The awareness of mankind is to be increased through the vibration of the heart. The heart absorbs the increased vibration in the form of energy from the sun, and avails it to the body. The sun in turn gets its increased energy from the Central Sun of the entire solar system.

With the increased energy in your body, your awareness awakens; your thinking and feeling are more intelligible, more liberal, and clearer. It is as though you emerge from the fog and see and understand everything around you better and more clearly. If also your intellect follows this path into the higher energy, your consciousness is awakened.

With the ascent into the higher frequency it is important that you accept the new energy; this, however, is only possible if the clarification and purification of the body took place in advance. All interrelationships of an energetic nature are perceived only through the increased awareness. Shaping life creatively is the consequence of all learning processes which preceded. For all human beings the ascent is a challenge for body, mind, and soul.

If you understand, implement, and live the process of ascension, it will take you to freedom on all levels. Your planet Earth is following the same path; the entire solar system and the galaxy are part of the ascension process.

Be aware of the powerful collective which is at work here and expedites the change of dimension.

Your planet wishes to include all people in its change of dimension, and with this text appeals for your understanding for the clarification processes, which are necessary.

At the same time, reading on and understanding the master power of Aurora, this text constitutes a strong increase of vibration to connect you with Mother Earth.

I am Lady Aurora. My energy is available to you children on Earth at all times in order to establish contact with your Earth, Gaia.
In love,
Aurora

Lady Rowena pursues the path of initiation into the new era

Greetings to you, my brothers and sisters on Earth.
I am Lady Rowena, the master of initiation of the inner path,
which each of you beloved children will embark on in this era.

From the onset of the last galactic cycles, the transformation of Earth has been determined to take place now. Living on Earth at present, you consciously incarnated to participate in these processes of transformation. Your soul chose to be here now, right now, on this planet. Therefore I welcome you most warmly. My explanations serve to help everybody with the development of their personal inner path of initiation.

The path of initiation is your soul's path of recollection of the origin and the knowledge regarding the understanding of universal interrelationships.

You spent many thousands of years in the darkness of the polarity of the Earth.

During these lives you were meant to experience polarity; these were lives devoid of harmony. Many lives characterised by deprivation lie behind you. Now you are all on the path of enlightenment, of recognising who you really are.

You consist of body, spirit, and soul.

Everybody perceives themselves as being a *body*.

The soul is what remains after death (passing on from Earth), the true *I*. The soul is your true identity. It contains all information, it constitutes all that you are. All your lives, your origin, your life purpose, and all experiences are stored in the consciousness of the soul, in the memory of the soul.

The spirit, spirituality, is the connection to the Central Sun of your galaxy and thus the origin of God, or *All-That-Is*.

Only the combination of body + spirit + soul is what constitutes a human being, and ensures its survival on Earth. If one level is missing, life on Earth comes to an end.

The body is unable to live without the soul. This is what you see in your so-called coma patients, those who have been in a coma for a long time. The soul has departed from the body and had withdrawn into the etherial field around your body (see illustration). From the etherial field, it is unable to animate the body; it is a break from life. A coma occurs when the body is suffering severely and the pain is unbearable for the soul. Then the soul withdraws into the etherial field, where the pain is not felt. For the soul, this withdrawal from the body is a means of evading what is unbearable at the emotional level. If the body heals, the soul can return into the body.

Illustration (see below):

The aura consists of various energy layers (moving outward):

1) The ethereal aura, the ethereal body, is like a second skin, approximately ten centimetres wide around the physical body. It bears the life force.

2) The emotional aura, the emotional body, is like a cloud around the whole body. It includes your emotions and character traits.

3) The mental aura, the mental body, is egg-shaped, slightly milky in appearance, and surrounds the body. It bears your thoughts and ideas; even the experiences are stored in this body, and can be accessed.

4) The spiritual aura, also called causal body, is the radiance of your soul. It is the energy body carrying the light of the divine in it and radiating it into the world. The radiance of this aura can stretch for kilometres.

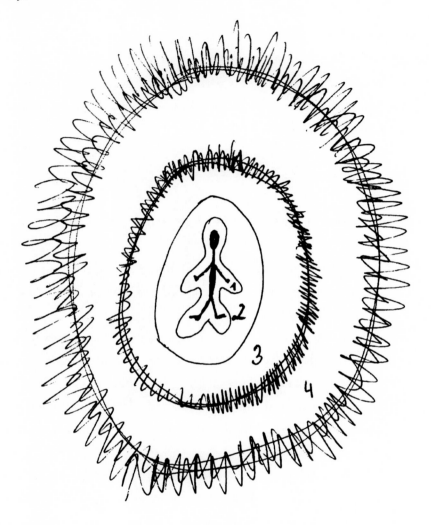

The soul is the 'helmsman' of your earthly body.

The body is the shell, the 'vehicle' on Earth, which enables the soul to learn and experience everything on Earth. When this earthly vehicle is defective, often irreparably, the soul rises from the body (the person dies) and *flies home*. For the soul, which is a small ball of light, home is a *monad*. These *monads* are soul groups which have complementary areas of learning and form a collective soul. This home, the monad, exists throughout the universe. The monads are purely spiritual connections of souls, and their locations are undetectable in the galaxies. These soul groups (monads) exist in the spiritual ether spheres only.

The spirit – which along with the body and the soul constitutes the human being – is the spark of God, without which life on Earth is impossible. Your idea of God, as interpreted by many of your religions, is an outdated concept with old visions.

For the new era, this old view should be corrected into multidimensionality. God, the Divine, is the all-pervading energy in all that exists. For your intellect, these statements are difficult to comprehend and to logically scrutinise. Up to this point in time, it was intentional that you on Earth did not understand God. Now, aimed at the 5th Dimension, spiritual doors representing a personal path to awareness for each of you, are being opened for mankind.

This path of initiation reveals a new understanding for the future. Recollections of the soul are being uncovered, hence correlations can be understood. It is an inward journey to the depths of your soul (creation of souls). We, the masters of spiritual energy, will gladly support you.

Previously, yogis spent a lifetime meditating to attain the wisdom of Buddha. Monks lived in monasteries to serve the Divine and to understand the way of the prophets and of the Son of God.

At any time on Earth, the inward journey was possible, usually connected with a life of celibacy and solitude, in silence. It was always possible for you to attain knowledge.

It has been planned that now, today and in the near future, every soul will awaken spiritually. Every person will recognise their Self, and draw the knowledge from the soul consciousness into their waking consciousness. With this recollection you will change; you will be able to understand the Divine.

The knowledge of your souls regarding the many incarnations will be accessible. Your origin, all correlations exceeding the time on Earth, will be revealed to your mind. Look forward to it because it means FREEDOM. Freedom for every soul, freedom on all levels.

Blame, guilt and related dependencies and fears will have no significance. The recognition of All-That-Is sets you free for ever. The constraints of your time are unimportant. Cast off the old! Life in the 5th Dimension is to be lived in freedom. The path of initiation which I teach, is the path to your Self.

The journey to the Self cannot be experienced in groups, seminars, through books, or on television. Everyone journeys by themselves; alone, it is a lonely path. It is important to listen to your inner voice (it is particular to you) and to follow it. Listening to the voice within requires great sensitivity and patience. Do not place pressure on yourself to succeed though you may wish to do so. Remember, everything takes time and everything always happens at the right time. You cannot force anything.

Once you have become used to listening to your inner voice, ask: who or what is speaking.

Ask after the name and for an explanation; ask incessantly, and you will be answered. You can ask questions on all aspects of life, the origin of the soul, seek explanations for a better understanding, etc. Once communication has been established, then trust!

You will be trained by the information you receive.

The voice which is in contact with you can be your Higher Self (the spiritual spark of God), a spirit guide, an angel, a priest, ascended masters, or beings from higher dimensions.

But those who make contact with you will introduce themselves and point out their origin and what connects them with you, why they are with you and why he/she is instructing you.

'Hearing' may also be a feeling or an inner knowledge for many people; each of you perceives individually, on different sensory levels.

Many of you also receive inner images which will guide you to Realisation.

As always, many paths lead to the same outcome.

Accept your path, for it is your personal journey to your Self, to your 'I Am', to the divine spark in you. Only, and really only by realising who you really are, will you find the answers to life and to the future. Through the changes which affect you personally, you therefore energetically assist in organising the ascent into the 5th Dimension.

This book came into being because the voices of the ascended masters were heard and recorded in writing; the energetic work of translating it into the English language has made it more comprehensible for the reader.

Have the courage and the confidence to take the path of initiation, of self-realisation, for your liberation from the constraints of the past.

In freedom, step into the future confidently.
This I wish from the depth of my heart.
With love to all souls on Earth,
Lady Rowena

Master El Morya describes the process of the evolution of the heart

God be with you, you children of Earth.
Turquoise energy rays touch your hearts and make my announcements
intelligible.
I Am Master El Morya. My text informs you about the evolutionary
process of the heart.

The human heart is the control centre of the body, for emotions associated with the love of the universe, the all-encompassing love of God and the universal intelligence of the Central Sun. This intelligence is inherent in every soul and is the spark which constitutes your existence as a human being on planet Earth.

The conditions for life on Earth, the preparations for the soul's life on Earth, have been deleted from your memory, and are thus not accessible to you. Your life in the body with the carrier of intelligence (the mind) is seemingly empty. Actually, this is not so!

When your soul entered your body (the decision to be born as a human), it deleted the memory of its origin and other information too. The soul, when reborn, cannot remember its previous lives.

Only by living, by experiencing, and creating, do hunches, forebodings, and inexplicable knowledge surface – you call it wisdom.

When this happens to them, people say they are on the path to God, on their spiritual path. Wisdom is gained by unconsciously remembering the sum of experiences of previous lives, or their essence.

- Being on the path to God,
- being on the spiritual path,
- walking on the path of compassion,
- feeling and living the love with others,
- the need to understand oneself,
- searching for the meaning of life, is the key to the door of your soul.

This is the only way to open the door to memories of previous lives.

The time being experienced on Earth now is very special. It makes it possible for many people to follow this path of recollection of their own accord.

We from the spiritual world guide you, but it is the high energy reaching the Earth at present which makes this development possible. You may wonder how your thoughts and feelings have changed. You cannot exactly recall *when* you started thinking and behaving differently - it simply happened. This is the onset of change, which is brought about by the increase of energy in every person and of the entire planet. Look forward to this renewal and accept it. None of you, even though they may brace themselves strongly against this process of awareness, will remain unaffected.

In the future, the thoughts of all human beings will evoke feelings in the heart.

When lingering in this feeling, you notice that it is different. This emotion from your heart moves you very deeply, and you notice how overwhelmed you are by your own emotions. Many people will try to question this wave of emotion intellectually, but will encounter inexplicable limits. Please accept this boost of emotional feelings and give in to it. The cause, the emergence of the tenderness in your energized heart, can arise from the sight of a child, a beautiful sunset, a lovely journey, etc. Though you have often witnessed these, they suddenly touch you deeply. This strong wave of emotion right into your heart will rouse your energy system, the aura and the body. Only then will you be able to analyse old conflicts, the origin of your constant anger, or why you always react the way you do. Now you can heal old wounds, reconsider past life situations and release them, and finally clarify issues and resolve problems. Clearing your behavioural and emotional world is necessary because your heart wishes to lighten itself and enter into the higher frequency free from ballast.

The strong emotions are meant to increase the energy level of the heart and induce energy surges into the systems of the body. This gradually leads to an increase in frequency in every cell and thus increases the energy in the body as a whole. When somebody strives for an increased awareness and simultaneously seeks a holistic way of life, the energy process at a physical level can be stepped up. The increased frequency heals all physical diseases. This healing is a chemical process which is automatically initiated by the increased energy, by the light in the body.

Before healing can take place, the physical cleansing of the human organism must be completed.

This phase of transition produces various physical symptoms; these reach from the cleansing processes of the systems of the body to pain caused by tension, or the total collapse of the body. Your doctors can hardly explain these processes and in most cases do not understand the physical process as being a necessary check of the system. This will change over the years; the increased awareness will offer new healing methods, which will be implemented.

An example of the new way of healing: images with a high frequency consisting of colours and shapes, representations of beautiful natural scenes, or pictures of angels already exist today. Placed on the body or meditated upon, they have healing energies, which, when the viewer allows it, will heal the body and the soul.

The heart is the body's control centre radiating energy. It works together with the brain, your computer. The radiation of your heart's emotions is communicative impulses perceived by humans, animals, plants, and the whole universe. They are understood as information from the subconscious mind.

With your heart energy, on the subtle level (energy level), you also communicate with each other. Sometimes you say: Someone has charisma, or they have a good heart. This information is transmitted from the heart and perceived by others, subconsciously. In future, the subconscious perception will turn into conscious perception; then you will understand more of what is going on around you.

The physical heart remains the pump distributing the blood throughout the body.

On the subtle level – the different auras surrounding the body – the heart functions as the carrier of the soul energy and conveys information on the spiritual level. An exchange from soul to soul, with the help of the heart energy, can be understood by everyone. This exchange on the energetic level will change your social systems. Empathising will cause humans to change, and thus the Earth, too. Each of you exudes sensitivity and touches the hearts of other human beings with your heart energy, and they in turn receive it. Many of you respond with your hearts in this way. In so doing, the Earth will gradually undergo the process of increasing its energy and finally reach the 5th Dimension. This change is unstoppable. It already started years ago.

When the heart frequency becomes finer and communication more sensitive, then new areas of perception will open up to you.

Due to the increase of energy, your body systems will reach a higher frequency. Thus you will be able to get in touch with the energies of the world of fairies and dwarves, the Ascended Masters, angels, unicorns, and the spirits of nature.

Owing to this sensitive communication, this book came into being.

Through her heart energy, this channel agreed to assume contact with the energy of the Ascended Masters of the 'White Brotherhood', and of the 'Karmic Board of the Earth'. Thus we, from the spiritual world, used this frequency to direct our *MESSAGES* to humanity through her, and to create this book.

Through this book, we spiritual masters instruct you and establish contact between you and the new energy. But we also want to teach you so that you can understand what is happening to Earth and to humanity.

This textbook is meant to address your intellect in order to explain what is happening, in the hope that you will be able to accept the present process of development more easily. Understanding the processes facilitates accepting the energetic changes.

Reading these texts from the spiritual world raises your energy; you will understand more consciously. With the translation of these texts into the English language by the other channel (she agreed to channel the energy of the Masters of the spiritual world into these texts once more), the frequency of the information is increased, and the instruction is energetically accelerated.

The combination of these frequencies makes this book unique.

Repeated reading of these texts (the book) is advisable, as this will increase the energy in the body systems steadily, and the awareness of your thoughts and feelings will be heightened.

In the future many people will be able to get in touch with us, from the spiritual world. This energy teaches you!

You will be able to communicate with all spirit beings.

When you become aware of our presence, accept and perceive it, and pay attention to us, your life will be easier, lighter, and joyful.

The energetic information, the energetic exchange between the human, earthly world and the light, spiritual beings, helps you to attain more clarity, and to understand the world as a whole.

Dare to do so. We desire interaction with all of you, for the benefit of the entire universe.

In divine and infinite love to all humans, and more particularly to those reading these words, I, EL Morya, Master of the turquoise ray of love, bless you.

Lady Kuan Yin guides into compassionate love

May God's mercy bless you!
I, Lady Kuan Yin, Master of Compassion, address you.
My mantra is Om mani padme hum.

The cultures on Earth are mixing, indicating you are all O*ne*, consisting of: body – mind - spirit. In the past there have been many ramifications of cultures and religions on Earth. The intergalactic influences of the universe materialised creating this cultural diversity on Earth. The illusion of diversity is now irrelevant in the new era, the emergence of the future energy of light.

You may stop distinguishing between colour, religion, culture, men and women, for gender is irrelevant in the 5th Dimension. Be aware that only the composition of your existence is important, namely

* body (the force of Mother Earth)
* spirit (the divine spark, the universal light of life)

* and soul (your spark of light, the personal memory card of your individual life, of all incarnations).

These bases of your being are the same for all people on Earth. This knowledge concerning the sameness of the human species should unite you as a group.

In the 5th Dimension you will get to know other species and will get in touch with them. Look forward to the interaction, it will be rewarding at all levels.

In the animal kingdom, all species recognise one another and respect each other unconditionally. With the consciousness of unity, you too should recognise one another and accept each other.

With pleasure you recognise the individual strengths and abilities of other people, and despite the differences you feel united as a group of humans.

At the energy level the recognition of this bond is supported by the compassion for other people. Compassion is heartfelt love and can alleviate suffering in individuals and in entire groups. The mantra (chanting, which increases energy) of compassion is *Om mani padme hum*, which comes from the ancient Sanskrit writings of the Tibetan people. The Indian, Thai, and other eastern cultures know this mantra of compassion. This mantra is a vibration which effects pain reduction at all levels by uttering, singing, thinking, or reading. The energy frequency is activated and spreads like the rays of the sun. Mantras, sung or spoken in a group, are energy waves which can spread for miles, and their effect there is noticeable.

Compassion means I empathise with and support the energy that everything may turn out for the best.

Pity means I support the energy of suffering by co-suffering.

The compassion in your heart joins you together and makes love flow – to the benefit of all. This feeling unites mankind to act responsibly.

Earlier, in days gone by (in some regions today too) the monks, including those awakening spiritually, chanted and sang the mantra of compassion in order to feel the vibration in the heart and to experience the strength and confidence this energy releases. On the spiritual level, compassion was sent to countries, cities, people, and war zones so that peace and love could flow to mitigate disasters and to let hope grow.

Today, the Earth has a higher frequency so that information flows faster. You know how quickly information is sent around the world by computer or mobile phone. Spiritual energy is similar. It manifests much faster and reaches its destination faster. Hours of mantra singing to increase the energy have become unnecessary. Today, just thinking a mantra is enough to let energy flow wherever it is needed.

Due to the increased light vibration on your planet, faster information and energy transmission is possible. Thoughts flow faster from sender to receiver and also reach their destination, irrespective of whether they were thought consciously or subconsciously.

It is very easy for all of you to actively live a life of compassion and to regard your thoughts and actions as a unified life, worldwide. The thoughts of compassion projected onto a particular situation can affect it positively.

Simply stated: Heartfelt love can be applied to the benefit of world events; its effect is always positive. For inexperienced people, it is easier to generate an energy wave by using the frequency of compassion. The energy of love is deeper and requires a greater awareness. However, both energies always act exclusively for the benefit of all people and situations involved.

Example: Thinking or saying the mantra whilst passing the scene of an accident (rescuers at scene), clarification or improvement will set in for all involved.

Compassion always leads to great divine benefit for all concerned; it takes suffering from the occurrences. Energetically, suffering is transformed into promise and hope.

Compassion unites you and inspires you to treat each other more humanely, regardless of religion and culture, or money and status.

Mother Earth needs humane people on her surface in order to be able to continue her existence.

You need compassion for each other in order to notice and appreciate your equality.

The heart in the human body is the centre of energy. The heart supplies the body with blood and everything it needs. When the heart shuts down, the body is incapable of living. But the heart is also the centre of energy for the emotional body. It is responsible for your feelings. A feeling develops, arises in the heart chakra, and can be physically sensed via the nerves. Feeling is the energetic task of the heart.

The feeling of love comes straight from the heart centre, the heart, and as you say it can 'move mountains'. This is a human expression for the force that arises from the feeling of love. The energy of love for 'All That Is' shows the way to the 5th Dimension, to the ascent of the planet, to the kingdom of peace on Earth – which has been praised for ages.

Loving, spontaneously from your heart, you associate with living together in a partnership, or love to your children, your parents, or sometimes even your pets.

Loving means opening your heart centre.

But to *whom* and for *what* do you want to open your innermost centre?

According to the divine understanding, for 'All That Is'. For your fellow human beings, for situations in which you find yourself, for yourself in the very first place, for Mother Earth, for your enemies and adversaries, for the unresolved past, for animals, for nature, for the suffering of your planet, and much more. You see, in terms of love there is something for each of you. To open one's heart for something or to someone requires thorough cleansing.

This is the reason why planet Earth, at present, is so 'cool' and often inhumane.

The masses on Earth distrust the feeling of love and rely on the reasoning of the brain. For many of you, opening one's heart means revealing oneself and being vulnerable. In many partnerships you are controlled and your heart is closed – towards your children you are often heartless. You imagine this to be an important learning area in your society which is controlled by money and power. This belief makes you rigid and thus leads to the inhumane excesses of your present society.

I, Kuan Yin, from my divine heart, in the all-embracing love, appeal to you to change your behaviour and to open yourselves to love.

In the first place, love yourself (free of self-centredness). Accepting and loving yourself as you are, with all your faults and strengths, is a major challenge. Dare, dare to love yourselves. Then you will be amazed at the great potential available to you through self-love. It causes you to change, you believe in yourself again, you can even heal yourself, and much more. Trust yourself by opening up to love!

Then open yourself to love persons close to you. You will notice that the relationships among you will change positively when love flows.

When you are experienced, open up to the world and to all that lives on Earth, and to the great soul Gaia.

You will create your world anew using love and an open heart, and thus fashion your planet into the kingdom of peace.

Begin with yourself, dare to love, and be lovable. When thousands of people open themselves in this way, confidence and reliability will be renewed on your planet due to the energy which flows from the heart.

Some of you have been living in accordance with the new patterns of love, but these numbers must increase in the years to come. For the Earth is ascending and wishes to take as many people with it, but this can only happen in the energy of love. It is so simple: just love yourself, and everyone else too. Abandon judging and evaluating. Do understand that you are all *one*, you all belong to the human species. Accept each other with all your weaknesses and recognise that each of you has come to Earth to learn. No one is perfect, otherwise you would not be here.

In the next few years, the main area of learning for you, on Earth, will be to open your heart and to increase the energy of love. Only in this way will the societies of your countries transform for the benefit of all people and continents.

Everything which was conceived, built and created in love will persist in the light of the 5th Dimension. Please recognise this and take it as a given.

I, Kuan Yin, convey this text with great love for the whole of humanity and with the hope of change, under the banner of the divine energy of the heart, the All-embracing Love.

20

Sanat Kumara directs the eternal quality of Time on Earth

I Am Sanat Kumara. I direct the Earth at present.
I most heartily salute the divinity in all human souls.

My remarks will help you to understand

* the time on Earth now,
* how to imagine the ascent into the higher light frequency,
* and how to fulfil your soul purpose.

You humans have been reborn many times and have experienced many things during your lives on Earth. The repetition of lives now comes to an end. The current time on the planet heralds the end of experiences as you have hitherto lived through. In the years to come, the Earth slowly ascends to a higher energy level, and many souls too will ascend to the new frequency, into the 5th Dimension. The learning processes on Earth come to an end. In the future, on the new level permeated with light, you will be able to have very different experiences. The Earth rises into lighter spheres and thereby renews itself. The cleansing process takes place before the ascension and is already under way.

You have lived many lives, separate from the knowledge of who you really are. The polarisation of your material world into 'black' and 'white' poles has influenced your human experience. This duality comes to an end with the energy of light which radiates more strongly from the Central Sun onto the sun and thus onto Earth – and which is responsible for the ascent of the planet. The new presence of light, emanating from the Central Sun, changes the entire galaxy. All 'shadows' will show up (be lit up), manipulations and other intrigues can no longer escape the light. The new light penetrates the shadows and removes blockages and congestions, at all levels. You notice it in your daily lives. The light presence of the spiritual world shines through all areas of your life and changes it for the better. Faltering processes are set in motion and resolve in the light, changing into clear, new ideas and concepts. These changes trigger healing in all areas, bringing freedom and ease into your lives. Absorb the divine light of the sun and set off on your way to an easier life in harmony.

As soon as the cleansing processes are over (this will take a few years) and the old system has collapsed, you will be able to create new social systems and shape a life in harmony with the new-found peace among you.

Warfare on Earth then belongs to the past because old strife was resolved in light. You do not allow yourselves to be manipulated because the light sees through the dalliances and makes them unattractive.

Living in pure energy gives the body a lighter vibrancy.

Food too will be easier to digest as you will prefer a Mediterranean diet.

The mental abilities become more sensitive and contact between humans, as well as between humans and animals will gradually reach the stage of telepathy. This novel way of sensing your body will make the spiritual world visible. You will recognise your spirit guides and contact them directly receiving clear spiritual help from them personally, in conversation. Many things will become clearer when the veils (energy) between the worlds are lifted and you will be able to see what had previously merely been hopes and beliefs. You will be able to peer at the subtle worlds beyond the energy veil. Gradually, very gradually, step by step, otherwise it would be too demanding for you. You will understand and accept what many of you imagined to be fiction or fantasy only. There are already people who can see beyond the veil of dimensions, unfortunately they are only a few. These people are misunderstood by society and portrayed as 'crazy', but in a few years you will laugh at the thought.

Of course, there are souls who are not going to ascend, for every soul can choose independently.

With their earthly areas of learning, these souls will remain in a parallel universe. This universe is an illusion of the past, built after the model of the Earth in the 3rd Dimension. Yes, that is the way things are. In this dimension, these souls can continue working on their earthly learning areas; they can always reincarnate until they too are ready for ascension into the lighter dimensions.

Intellectually, this parallel universe is difficult to conceptualise because it is merely a big 'soap bubble', which, as universe, is available for a limited time only. When, eventually, it is no longer needed, it will explode and become light. The incarnate souls in the 'soap bubble' may take their time to complete their learning areas. And how do these souls get into the bubble? Many people die on Earth and incarnate on the parallel Earth; others move on in a sleeplike state, while others step into the old world in a dream. Each soul chooses the path best suited.

Those (hopefully many!) who choose to ascend with the earth energetically, will (partly unconsciously but with relief) notice that 'times' are improving and that living conditions are becoming better and easier. Other ascending souls receive the new energy consciously, immersing into it in a sleeplike state. Still others awaken from a disease or a feverish flu, feeling like a newborn person in the new energy. Some souls pass through the energy gate to the 5th Dimension in stages, ridding themselves of one blockage after another until they feel free and renewed, and accept the high frequency of light as their life energy. There are other models of ascension; every soul has brought its own personal plan for this lifetime.

Now the time has come; step by step, you will be guided to your particular soul plan of awakening, and thus into the energy of the 5th Dimension. In accordance with their consciousness, each one will either ascend or return to the experiences of the polar plane, to Earth.

I Am Venus in the form of energy,
and I come to your Earth with the feeling of love
in order to support the children of mankind in the
process of ascension into the frequency of light.

Light and love will steer the turn of the eras into the higher spheres.

Love is the energy of the heart and designs everything thought and sought absolutely positively. With love, disharmony is converted into harmony.

In the third Dimension of the Earth, achieving harmony among people was a sought-after goal.

Now, with the high frequency of the light of the 5th Dimension, the aim is achieving unity and perfection. This new aim becomes possible with the help of the energy increase, and the path will have to be a spiritual one. It leads to unity with God.

The knowledge concerning unity in Divine Light was predicted thousands of years ago in your religious scriptures. This time has now dawned.

Becoming one with the Light, completely aware, the immersion of the body and the soul in divinity, and thus bringing the wheel of reincarnation to a halt – this time has now dawned.

Becoming one with 'All That Is', knowledge of the God-head, the Central Sun, returning to the origin of the soul, overcoming separateness, and thus detecting all the machinations of the dark side, turning one's back on darkness, and joyfully living in the light of 'Oneness' - that is the new life.

Perfection on all levels of being, becoming one with the consciousness of the 'I AM Presence' (the divinity of every human being), is possible now, with love and light.

This message guides you into the new energy of the 5th Dimension.

Spiritual guides and the angelic beings teach and prepare you for Oneness. It will be an evolutionary process as it was in the past, in the

3rd Dimension. Here too, each soul individually decides the schedule in which the processes are to take place. Thus, exactly like this, the learning areas will develop in the energy of light, in the 5th Dimension, with the frequency of Divinity, towards Oneness with the only 'One'.

The energetic frequency of this text is very high. Therefore the text should be read more than once to open the gates of your system even wider to let in the photonic light, and love.

With great respect for your human performance in the past and the forthcoming processes of ascension into the high energy frequency, I bless you, children of mankind, with divine confidence and growing wisdom.
The director of time,
Sanat Kumara,
and Venus.

Master Serapis Bey illuminates the dark

I Am Serapis Bey, a spiritual master. On the glistening, white ray of light, I assist with the clarifying and liberating processes on Earth. I illuminate all darkness and guide you into the Divine Light, the new frequency of light on Earth.

My energy reaches you for I am with you, and with my light I escort you. God be with you!

My messages to you:

Dare to journey to the freedom of the divine light, get on your way, leave the old structures behind, and have the courage to accept the change - the expansion of your consciousness. All efforts will be rewarded. You will be liberated, and emerge from darkness into light. Do proceed with confidence!

Life will have a new quality. In the 5th Dimension, harmony will be lived actively, and will lay the foundation for the path of the enlightened perfection of your souls.

In a short time, the new dimension which will be achieved by Mother Earth will open unimaginable possibilities for you. You will learn to use energy as a means to create, and will appreciate it. Dealing with the energy of the new era will create many new ways of utilising it, which in the 3rd Dimension was impossible. Generating energy from solids (wood, oil, etc.) was right for Earth at the time. But now energy will occur in a different form. It can be compared with fog - it is visible and yet invisible. Once your body and its aura have adjusted to the energy of the lighter dimension, you will be able to understand and direct the fog. The energy of the new light frequency is adaptable: It can be focused in order to shape, warm, cool, or build. It will simply be a raw material for your new communities. Producing energy from fossil fuels to generate power and heat will be a thing of the past. The light energy is there; it has a consciousness and can be used to generate heat, power, and much more. The consumption of matter as is needed on Earth now becomes unnecessary. A few of your scientists, whose consciousness has already acknowledged the light energy, have been working enthusiastically on the implementation of the new light quality. Your societies are still impervious regarding engineering the light. This will change in the next few years when the mass consciousness of the people increases, rises. Thus, there will be no life of procurement any longer as practiced in the material world of the 3rd Dimension. The light energy of the new era is always present – everywhere; you take it and use it to design articles needed for daily use. Quite simply: form air or fog, give the energy an assignment. Direct the awareness of the energy where it is needed, simply by thinking.

Presently, this text may appear visionary, but time marches on, and soon you will comprehend the truth of these statements.

Be patient, everything happens according to a divine plan. With this information, I jolt your powers of imagination and would like to open up your perspective for visions.

Light is energy vibrating at a high frequency moving constantly. This high frequency of energy is also present in love, divine thinking, meditation, healing, and in many areas of life where this invisible energy is utilised. This invisible quality will become visible in the new dimension; then you will see what is now only believed and accepted as real.

Everything is energy: angels, fairies, gnomes, nature spirits, spiritual masters.

Thoughts are invisible, but they are energy.

Visions and dreams are invisible, but they too are energy.

Sun rays are invisible, but palpable energy.

Light is visible, but energy devoid of solid particles (impalpable); it is an energy which is transparent, diffuses in space, and expands.

The new dimension challenges your intellect, but with the increased spirituality in your body cells, and your expanded consciousness it will be comprehensible.

A long time ago already, your ancient scriptures prepared you for this turn of eras, now the time is truly come. The transition is taking place, but not suddenly; it will take years to accomplish the transition process itself. In the 5th Dimension, the phase of settling in will encompass several hundred years (according to your current perception of time). The Earth will not be jerked into the new energy, like with a pistol shot; but the energy will rise gradually until the high frequency can be sustained constantly. You are already experiencing the variability of energy: the general hustle and bustle is palpable, the rapid changes in almost all areas of life are noticeable, the racing quality of time is experienced; such is life in the 4th Dimension; it is restless and changeable.

We from the spiritual world are prepared to assist everyone, if so desired.

By reading the texts in this book, you are being trained and energetically prepared for the transition.

I, Serapis Bey, often heard the thoughts of people with a higher awareness. One of the most common questions was 'how'.

How are our societies to become more transparent?
How is the power of money to lose its importance?
How will the power games on Earth come to an end?
How will social justice be implemented?
How will we be able to feed all people on Earth?
How will lasting peace on Earth be possible?

And many, many more 'hows'.

This question of 'how' comes from the mind. It requires explanations in order to open the energy pathways of the body to receive the light frequency. Blockages (which the mind sees because something appears inexplicable) must be released so that the increased frequencies of light can promote the expansion processes in the body cells.

In a galaxy light vibrations often vary in intensity, and it is no different in yours.

The Earth has two polar energies. It is dominated by these two energies, which are equally important. This polarity is a great learning environment for many souls who incarnate on Earth. The two dominant poles are :

* the energy of the divine, heavenly light, a high frequency
* and the solid, power-oriented, low frequency of the dark side.

This Earth is special in that two opposing energies can be experienced here, which is a very rare learning situation in the galaxies. In the spirituality of the universe (where judgment is foreign), Earth is regarded as a 'nursery' for souls. Here you are allowed to play around with both energies, and then eventually, after many lifetimes, you decide to follow the light. For the dark side is an illusion, which exists in the 3rd Dimension on Earth.

Energetically, the dark side is a cul-de-sac. On the dark side, there is no expansion, no advance; you can only return to the light. Your soul, the divine spark in you, comes from the light of God and needs the divine light in order to grow and create.

The dark side is a learning environment to train yourself to sense your experiences, physically and at all other levels. The dark side offers no future, it holds you back and becomes rigid; it is not transparent. When looking closer, the energy of darkness is manipulative and dominant; initially, however, it seems understanding and accepting. This guise of being the light in order to veil, to cover the darkness, inspires many people. This game is almost always based on seduction, delusion, lies, and mystifying people, enticing them into the dark. It is a game which, at present, is being pursued on Earth to the full, and which reveals many facets.

The selfishness in the human system prefers to believe the dark side, and feels good when assured that it is more beautiful and better, smarter and richer than all other people. The temptation to rise above others is great because your social systems apparently reward all those at the top. Living on Earth, i.e. enjoying everything with paradisiacal conditions reigning, is seductive – and this is a promise of the energy of darkness. It is an illusion which can be enjoyed at first; but then the dark side demands gratification; it demands nurturing and proliferation, and expansion in order to gain power. Thus the dark side promotes manipulative, deceitful machinations in escalating dimensions.

These experiences of darkness are intended in the world of polarity; it is a trying out of the two energies – light and darkness.

The dark energy works independently with the appropriate awareness, and acts against the light. The consistency of the low-vibrating shadows is firmer and inert. They can adjust well and assume many different forms and facets (cheeky, friendly, encouraging, brash, brutal, flattering, etc.). That is why mankind lived such complicated lives in the past – always torn between the two energies. Distinguishing between the poles is difficult even today. You sense the light as being easy, loving, touching, healing, reliable. The dark side, with its many disguises, reveals its many facets. In most cases, the dark energy unmasks itself whenever it believes to have won over the ego, i.e. a human being. Then the demands begin to intensify: the power play, the lies, the manipulation, and gaining other souls for this lifestyle.

The dark side is interested in power, domination and expansion. I appeal to you to read these explanations without judgment because together with the spiritual beings planet Earth has provided these learning areas. These learning experiences are the will of God. In the past, the Earth was thus a training location of inter-galactic interest, and was attended and enlivened by extra-terrestrials who also wanted to try this unique experience. Today, in this era, the former energy gates have been closed; they are guarded by Ashtar Sheran's cosmic squadron to ensure the uninterrupted ascension of the Earth through the turn of the eras into the 5th Dimension.

Your wars and battles have been power games of the dark side.

Now, currently, the power play is in full swing on your planet. It is fought subtly in the form of monetary power. Worldwide large sums of money are being pushed back and forth; few people and organisations enrich themselves at the expense of the rest of the world. The dark side plays its game with great pleasure and power; many rich people worship it and earn well by the money transactions around the globe. The supervision of the game machinations has long escaped world politics. Restriction becomes difficult and seems hopeless. It would appear that the dark energy has entirely taken possession of the Earth. And exactly this is the intention in order to attract as many players as possible. This impression is deceptive. The bulk of the world's population is not involved in these great power plays. They are struggling for survival in the anti-social societies. Distracting the masses by the struggle for survival is also part of the game.

The media fuel the game of money and authority in that they publicise, via television and the newspapers, the impression that those who do not participate in this game have themselves to blame, and belong to the weak, to the needy in society.

All these are manoeuvres of the dark side. It is incredibly active on your Earth. It gains ground quickly and manipulatively as if fighting for survival. Well, that is the way it is: the survival of the dark side is at stake.

The new light penetrates everything which is still solid and non-transparent, even the dark. The energies, it would seem, are at war. The question is:

Which energy will remain? In the 5th Dimension, the energy of the dark side will not endure. The divine light will penetrate and dissolve it. Consequently, the dark consciousness fears its demise. It must fight against the light, otherwise the dark will simply dissolve.

The consciousness of light is waiting to see how the dark side will behave. It is watching to see what cunning the dark side will invent.

To you it seems as if the light is absent and as if the shadows have taken possession of the Earth. The light operates quietly and brings the power of transparency, in which nothing, absolutely nothing, remains hidden. Take heed, many manipulations are already being revealed, being seen through, and are dissolving on their own. Be patient and hold on to the hope of the light. Your Earth and the machinations on and in it will be cleared. You humans are living through an interesting period. It is exciting to participate so openly in the game of Dark against Light. For each of you fights the fight within yourselves, within your own mind and body.

Your consciousness can be sharpened by distinguishing between the two polar energies. Recognising the energies is the learning task in your present time. The ability to distinguish Light from Dark is the greatest challenge you have to face as a whole, as the human race. Start the journey, dare to recognise, then decide. This process, your decision, is important for the change of dimensions.

In the 5th Dimension the dark energy cannot endure. Polarity is non-existent there. Polarity only exists in the 3rd Dimension, in the past and in the future.

Those souls who still want to try out the polar fields of learning, will find themselves in the parallel, illusory world (bubble), or incarnate there. There, in the new old world, you are allowed to continue living in the learning conditions of the Earth.

Each of you is free to choose; you will not be judged; the human will is to be accepted. Humans and the spiritual world must accept it. Every decision is good in itself!

It is important that a decision be made because going 'back and forth' cannot persist in the 4th Dimension. The turn of eras (the present time) is the time of decision for every soul on Earth.

The energy of the divine light allows the attack from the dark side because it is only a question of time before the light has permeated all machinations. The light illuminates the shadows, unmasks them, sees through them. This is a fact and cannot be manipulated.

In the turbulent, multi-faceted 4th Dimension, the Dark can still exist; it is combative, it wants to survive. During the transition into the 5th Dimension, it dissolves because the high frequency of light sees through it.

It dissolves in the Light and turns into Light. Thus, the shadow is illuminated in the light of God, and enters into the Divine Being.

Polarity does not exist in the light frequency of your future.

Polarity is the illusion of the energy of the 3rd Dimension.

Please have a look at yourself and see where darkness is still firmly anchored in the body systems. Here too, the process also takes place within. Flood yourself with light, and the thoughts and patterns of darkness will show up in the light, for darkness becomes visible in the presence of light. Often these are thoughts and patterns from the past. Please cast them off!

Call me by name. From the energetic plane, I will help you to dissolve the darkness in your systems. It is important that old patterns are cast off and released lovingly. Even the idea of 'feeling guilty about…' may be released here and now, and handed over to the divine light; they are hereby dissolved.

This releasing exercise may help you:

> *Please light a candle,*
> *be still, relax,*
> *then, call my name - Serapis Bey.*
> *Sense my clear, brilliant energy*
> *and name the patterns and thoughts to be cast off.*
> *Breathe deeply, three times,*
> *then think of what it is you want to cast off*
> *and blow it out loudly along with the air.*

Let go!
Now take your leave from me and extinguish the candle.
Expelling air should be repeated with each pattern or
thought until you have the feeling of being relieved and cleansed.
You can repeat this as often as you wish.

What is important is to practise controlling your thoughts thereafter. You should not allow the old patterns back into your systems by thinking about them.

When you let go of these patterns/thoughts, they disappear from your system, aura and body. Thus you can cleanse your energy system and be free in future. Having cast off and cleansed the shadows in Divine Light, you should invest all your strength in shaping your future.

For your future in the high light frequency of the 5th Dimension, the liberated feeling of freedom is indispensable because the past and its shadows should remain where they came into being - in the 3rd Dimension.

A note to your Churches:

The systems of the Churches of the world are permeated and possessed by the energy of darkness. Strong transparency will be required to expurgate all the machinetions.

The pressure to bring to light all manipulations can only come from the people. The exposures will be made public gradually for there are many. Perhaps the continued existence of your Churches is questionable? The awareness of the new era awakens Divinity in everyone and helps you understand it. Interpreting God becomes unnecessary.

In your new future, each one will be responsible for their energetic self-control, of their own volition. You think and feel very clearly like little children do at present. This helps to promote a high measure of personal responsibility. It will be self-evident that you will all strive to be and remain morally and ethically clean (this can be compared to keeping your body clean).

The high photonic light will transform you all enabling you to feel the divine unity.

Life on Earth is going to change to the benefit of mankind.

Joy and peace will be lived, spreading inspiration.

Have patience, maintain hope in the divine light, the kingdom of peace is at hand.

With my light and love, I accompany you through the upcoming years of transition.

I am with you if you should need me.
Call my name, and I will gladly journey with you for a while.
God be with you.
Master Serapis Bey

A final word from Mother Mary to the children on Earth

You beloved children on Earth,
I once dwelt among you, in the person of
Mary, mother of Jesus Christ.

Your joys and sorrows are familiar to me,
the karmic burden of earthly life weighs heavily.
Now it will come to an end,
suffering and pain will pass away,
the time of liberation from all burdens has come.
Heaven has opened up
taking planet Earth with it into the spiritual spheres.

My comfort I send to all, on Earth,
in times of want and despair.

My love for ever reaches your heart,
in the hours of sadness and mourning.

Mother Mary

My hope I give
in these days of darkness on the Earth.

My confidence I wish you all
when doubt and fear prevail.

My strength I send
to heal your body.

My courage I send
to tread the path into the divine era on Earth.

My confidence I put in you on Earth.

May this text accompany you into the future of your planet.

The divine consciousness will expand you enabling you to understand everything, the relationships and the processes which are now taking place on the planet.
The pace now lived is fast-moving and hectic, followed by periods of calm and tranquility, appropriately balanced.
Prepare for the silent tranquility which will soon reach your Earth.
A powerful storm will bring silence, which will gently cover every living being on Earth.
For a short while, you will dream in a dazed state.
Your awakening will be peaceful and gentle.
Your body systems will have adapted to the vibration of spirit and light.
Every one will be in their appropriate places.
Your memory will fade; your old life will be like a film passing by on a screen.

You will be baptized in wisdom experiencing the knowledge of All That Is. Mankind will have matured during the dream, well prepared for their new life.

'I' will have changed into 'We'.

You will be allowed to accept the longing for accomplishment, a deep satisfaction in your heart.

The new cycle of Earth in your galaxy will have begun.

I focus all my loving confidence on you,
Mother Mary
I send you the love of my earthly lives and of my present spiritual life directly
into your heart.

I am Mother Teresa at the right side of the loving Mother Mary.
I extend my blessing across the entire world, embracing each child on Earth,
in the divine light, for healing to occur on all earthly planes.
Peace be with you. Om Sai Ram.

I am the spiritual energy of Princess Diana and accompany the loving
Mother Mary on the left.
For you, my soul sisters and brothers, the path is prepared for the era of
light. The spiritual hosts lead you gently through the period of transition.
The life of want and suffering now comes to an end. In freedom you will
immerge into the Unity of Being, with the divine vibrations of your souls.
The all-embracing love and inner peace in each of you
will be possible in the future.
My hope in the Divine, for peace on Earth,
lived in love and joy, I send to all people on Earth.

In conclusion ...

I am Sathya Sai Baba, Master of the Universe, Master of All That Is.

Fear not. I shall guide you through all travesties on your planet. Much is taking place which you are unaware of for it is not visible to the physical eye. But I hold you in the palm of My hand. I guide you safely to the other shore. Much has been said about the present time, much has been written. Fear abounds, understandably, for many are not prepared for the transition yet. Light and love await you on the other side. Peace and tranquillity. But first upheaval will prevail, it is the order of the 'day'. 'Day', 'time' has no meaning in eternity – does not exist.

The Holy Mother has much to do. She is very busy preparing herself for a new life in the light. She is casting off all that burdens her, holds her back – just as you are doing now. This has been prepared and has been awaited for a very long 'time'. And NOW is the time.

Enjoy your divinity. Know I am here – we are ONE.
Om Sai Ram

In gratitude

We, the soul sisters, are deeply moved to have been able to fulfil our promise to the spiritual world.

It was a very exciting experience to act as channels guided by the spiritual masters.

We wholeheartedly thank the spiritual world for the trust put in us.

In love and humility
Matamani & Sai Kumari

Matamani

In this life, Matamani is called Linda Kolshorn and lives in Germany with her family. Many lives have prepared her for this channeling. While training as a healer, she became aware of her medial abilities, her life purpose.

Matamani has the gift of contacting the spiritual masters and archangels, unicorns, gnomes and spirits of nature, and to obtain information.

In gratitude,
Master St. Germain

I taught at a primary school in Germany for thirty years.

In search of the meaning of life, the following were very helpful in discovering my medial abilities:

- training as a Reiki teacher,
- training as a Bach flower therapist,
- and training as a healer.

In presentations of Bach flowers, Reiki and semi-precious stones, I realised that the spiritual world often spoke through me.

I gave the 'Karmic Council' of the spiritual world my consent to write this book and to bring the desired messages to the people on Earth.

Within three weeks, the text was given to me on the island of Ameland (Netherlands).

The Ascended Master Saint Germain is the initiator of this book.

With great confidence I have committed myself to the spiritual world, and with great pleasure I am looking forward to future ventures.

L.Kolshorn@gmx.net

Sai Kumari

I, Beulah Schneider, had a Christian upbringing in South Africa and loved visiting the local Bible Club. I enjoyed the morning and evening devotionals as well as the Bible Studies at the many camps I attended.

As a school teacher, I came into contact with Christian, Muslim and Hindu families. I simply loved my young charges. Love has always been my driving force, and not religion.

Many years later, in a dream, I had a vision of Sri Sathya Sai Baba. I did not really know who He was. A few years later, I had the wonderful opportunity of visiting Him in India. Oh God, what an experience! The Light and Love which permeated my being was indescribable! I visited His ashram annually a few times before His departure in 2011. Baba has been my constant Guide and Guru, and I now channel His 'messages'.

Since living in Germany, I have been working as a physio/psycho-, and ayurveda therapist, as a spiritual councillor, and as a translator for English speaking gurus, and it is obvious that I am a mere conduit through which the wisdom flows.

Om Sai Ram

saikumari@t-online.de

Lightning Source UK Ltd.
Milton Keynes UK
UKOW04f1322051214

242689UK00004B/157/P